Aspects of Christianity

Jesus of Nazareth

Aspects of Christianity

Jesus of Nazareth

MICHAEL KEENE

Stanley Thornes (Publishers) Ltd

First published in 2000 by:
Stanley Thornes (Publishers) Ltd
Ellenborough House
Wellington Street
CHELTENHAM GL50 1YW
England

00   01   02   03   04   /   10   9   8   7   6   5   4   3   2   1

A catalogue record for this book is available from the British Library.

ISBN 0-7487-5286-2

Printed and bound in China by Dah Hua Printing Press Co. Ltd.

Page layout by Penny and Tony Mills
Illustrated by Richard Johnson and Steve Ballinger

Acknowledgements

With thanks to the following for permission to reproduce photographs and other copyright material in this book:

ASAP/*Aliza Auerbach*: p.21; CIRCA/*John Smith*: p.13; Alex Keene for all other photographs; Martin Sookias: p.39.

Scriptures quoted from the *Good News Bible* published by The Bible Societies/HarperCollins Publishers Ltd., UK, © American Bible Society, 1966, 1971, 1976, 1992.

Every effort has been made to contact copyright holders. The publishers apologise to anyone whose rights have been inadvertently overlooked, and will be happy to rectify any errors or omissions.

Note: Throughout the series BCE (Before Common or Christian Era) and CE (Common or Christian Era) have been used in place of the traditional BC and AD. The new terms are more acceptable to followers of non-Christian religions.

CONTENTS

Behind *the* story *of* Jesus

THE WORLD OF JESUS

- Jesus was born in the Middle Eastern country of Palestine in around 5 or 6 BCE.
- Jesus was brought up in Nazareth, in Galilee.
- The Romans controlled Palestine. Most Jews hated the Romans.

Jesus was born around 5 or 6 BCE in a small Middle Eastern country called Palestine (see picture B). Today this country is known as Israel, an old Jewish name for the country. The Romans had ruled over Palestine since 63 BCE. They were to remain in power for another four hundred years.

Galilee

Jesus was brought up in Galilee, at Nazareth, in the north of Palestine. Galileans were Jews but they spoke with a different accent to those Jews who lived in Judea, further south. The Galileans were very independent people. Sometimes the Romans found them rather difficult to control. Samaria lay in between Galilee and Judea. Both the Galileans and the Judeans hated the Samaritans. Galilee was surrounded by nations that were not Jewish. The people who lived in these nations were called Gentiles, as were all people who were not Jewish.

The Romans

The Jews had to obey Roman laws and pay Roman taxes. Many Jews hated being under Roman control. They wanted their country to be under the rule of God. Some of them rebelled against the Romans in 6 CE under the leadership of Judas the Galilean. The revolt was quickly stopped but the movement started by Judas, involving

A Where was Jesus brought up?

6

B By which name is Palestine better known today?

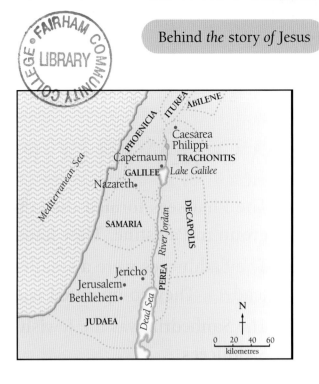

the Zealots, survived to the time of Jesus. One of the disciples of Jesus, Simon, was a Zealot.

Jesus did not seem to be against the rule of the Romans in Palestine. He certainly did not speak out strongly against it. This disappointed many Jews. Once, he was asked by some of them whether they should pay taxes to Rome. In his reply Jesus asked for a Roman coin. He asked the Jews whose name and picture was on the coin. They replied that it was the Roman emperor's. Jesus told them to give to the Roman emperor what belonged to him, the money, and to do the same with God (Luke 20.22–25).

The Jews and the Romans

Most Jews settled down to life under Roman power. They saw some of the benefits that the Romans had brought to their country – better roads, more trade, etc. To keep the Jews happy the Romans allowed them to have their own king and follow their own religion. The Romans did not usually interfere in this.

There were still many Jews, though, who were far from happy. They took part in a big Jewish revolt in 70 CE which the Romans stamped out ruthlessly. The Roman Army destroyed the Temple in Jerusalem, the holiest Jewish place, to teach the Jews a harsh lesson. Many Jews fled for their lives from Jerusalem, and Palestine, to live elsewhere in the Roman Empire. It was about this time that three of the four Gospels in the New Testament (Matthew, Mark and Luke) were written.

IN THE GLOSSARY

Disciple; Gentile; Gospels; Israel; Luke; Mark; Matthew; Nazareth; New Testament; Palestine; Temple; Zealots.

WHAT DO YOU KNOW?

1 a When was Jesus born?
  b What is the country of Jesus' birth called today?
  c Where was Jesus brought up?
  d Which country did both the Galileans and the Judeans hate?
  e What happened in 70 CE?

2 Look at the map (picture B). Find the same Middle Eastern countries on a modern map. Make a list of all the countries in picture B and the names by which they are known today.

3 a What did Jesus say when several Jews asked him whether they should pay taxes to the Romans?
  b Why do you think their question was a clever one?
  c What do you think Jesus wanted them to learn from his answer?

1 Behind *the* story *of* Jesus

TWO JEWISH GROUPS

- The Pharisees formed the largest, and most important, Jewish religious group in Palestine. They hated the Romans.
- The Sadducees were a smaller group which provided most of the religious leaders. They co-operated with the Romans.
- The Sanhedrin was the Jewish council made up of both Pharisees and Sadducees.

Jesus was a practising Jew. There were two important Jewish religious groups in Palestine during his lifetime. Their names crop up frequently in the Gospels. Almost always they were arguing with Jesus or plotting against him. These two groups were:

a The Pharisees. The largest religious group, the Pharisees, tried to keep

A A Pharisee stands behind Jesus in this Station of the Cross. Why do you think Jesus fell out with this group from the beginning?

themselves, and their religion, as pure as possible. The Pharisees would have nothing to do with Gentiles, or 'sinners' as they called them. They added many laws of their own to the Jewish Law, given by God to Moses, to protect it. These additional laws often made the lives of ordinary people a misery. This was one of the main reasons why Jesus fell out with them.

There were about 6,000 Pharisees in Palestine during the time of Jesus. They would not co-operate in any way with the Romans. Jewish men and women went to them for advice about the religious laws that they were expected to keep. The ordinary Jews looked up to the Pharisees and feared them. This made the Pharisees a very powerful group in Palestine.

b The Sadducees. The Sadducees were a much smaller group than the Pharisees. Most of the Sadducees were wealthy landowners and the Jewish leaders mostly came from this group. The High Priest, the leader of the Jews, was usually a Sadducee. Unlike the Pharisees, the Sadducees worked with the Romans rather than against them. They thought that they would get further by doing this.

B The Sanhedrin meets Why did the Romans allow the Jews to run many of their own affairs?

The Sanhedrin

The Sadducees and the Pharisees together made up the Sanhedrin. This was an important Jewish Council with 71 members which met in the outer Temple in Jerusalem. The Sanhedrin had the power to punish anyone who committed a religious crime against the Jewish faith. It played an important part in the death of Jesus.

An incident

In the Gospels the Pharisees and the Sadducees are often shown opposing Jesus. One incident involving them took place on the Sabbath Day. Some Pharisees were watching Jesus carefully since it was against their law to do any work on the holy day. A man with a paralysed hand came to Jesus to be healed. The religious leaders watched Jesus closely to see what he would do. They could not answer his question when he asked them whether their laws allowed someone to do good on the Sabbath Day. Jesus went ahead and healed the man, a good thing to do, but he made many enemies by his action (Luke 6.1–2; 6–11).

IN THE GLOSSARY
Gentile; Gospels; High Priest; Jerusalem; Moses; Palestine; Pharisee; Sabbath Day; Sadducee; Sanhedrin; Temple.

WHAT DO YOU KNOW?

1 a What were the two important Jewish religious groups in Palestine at the time of Jesus?

b Why did the Jews often go to the Pharisees?

c What was the main difference between the Pharisees and the Sadducees?

d What was the Sanhedrin and where did it meet?

2 Imagine that you had been born into the occupied country of Palestine. How do you think living under Roman occupation might have affected your daily life?

3 The Pharisees would have nothing to do with the Romans. The Sadducees co-operated with them. If you had lived in Palestine during the first century what do you think your attitude to the Romans would have been? Explain your answer.

1 Behind *the* story *of* Jesus

THE GOSPELS

- There are four Gospels in the New Testament.
- The Gospels provide us with almost all of our information about Jesus.
- The Gospels were written many years after Jesus left the earth.

The word 'Gospel' means 'good news' and was first used to describe the message that Jesus came to bring. He brought God's good news to the people, especially the poor. It was the poor who received him, and his message, with great excitement. Later the word was used for the books that tell us almost everything we know about Jesus. There are four Gospels in the New Testament – Matthew, Mark, Luke and John.

A How much time passed before the first Gospel was written?

Who and when?

None of the four Gospels actually tell us who wrote them. The names which they carry today were not given to them until the end of the second century. We cannot be sure just when they were written since the original manuscripts of each Gospel were lost a long time ago. Everything, though, seems to suggest that the first Gospel, Mark, was written around 65 CE. This was at least 35 years after Jesus had died in Jerusalem. The last Gospel, John, was not written until about 95 CE. By that time Jesus had been dead for 65 years.

What happened?

Why didn't the followers of Jesus write about him earlier? No one really knows. We can only guess. It could have been because:

- Every book had to be copied out by hand. This took a very long time. It was much easier to pass information around by word of mouth. Most of the stories about Jesus were kept alive by the disciples of Jesus preaching to the people and their words being remembered. Anyone who wanted to know about Jesus could ask his disciples for information. It was

B Why was it many years before the first Gospel was written?

only as the disciples grew old, and died, that the information needed to be written down before it was lost forever.

- For a long time the followers of Jesus thought that he would return to earth whilst they were still alive. He had promised them that he would do this. It was only when this did not happen that they began to write the information down.

- As the message of Jesus began to spread throughout the Roman Empire, and take a grip on the hearts and minds of the people, so many new Christians joined the Church. These people knew little about Jesus. A written record was needed so that they could read about Jesus for themselves.

The four Gospels in our Bible were not necessarily the first written records of Jesus. The Gospel writers may well have used earlier documents. If they did exist these early books have long since disappeared. Today the Gospels provide us with our only real information about Jesus.

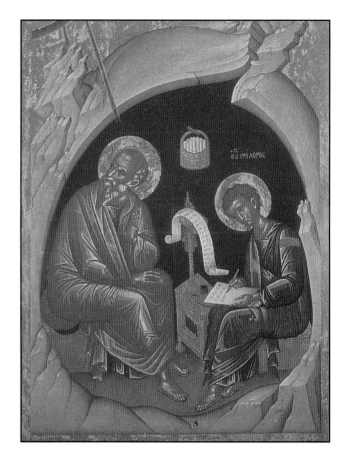

IN THE GLOSSARY
Disciple; Gospel; John; Luke; Mark; Matthew; New Testament.

WHAT DO YOU KNOW?

1 a How many Gospels are there in the New Testament?

b What are the names of the four Gospels?

c What does the word 'Gospel' mean?

d When were the first, and the last, Gospels thought to have been written?

e How was the information about Jesus passed around before the first Gospel was written?

2 Imagine that you were a convert to the Christian religion in the years following the death of Jesus. How do you think you might have heard about Jesus in the first place?

3 You are a Christian leader in the first century. Other leaders at the time believe that it would be a good idea to write down all that is known about Jesus but you resist them. What arguments would you put forward for your point of view – and how might you have changed your opinion as time went on?

Behind *the* story *of* Jesus

JESUS

- The four Gospels describe Jesus being baptised in the River Jordan.
- Jesus taught the people by using parables. He also performed many miracles.
- Jesus enjoyed a last meal with his disciples before being put to death by the Romans.

Two of the four Gospels, Matthew and Luke, begin their story of Jesus with his birth in a stable in Bethlehem. The other two, Mark and John, do not mention this but start with Jesus preaching in Galilee.

A   A church, part of the worldwide Christian Church. Which group of people established the Church after the death of Jesus?

All four of them then move from his teachings and miracles through to his death on a cross in Jerusalem and his resurrection from the dead.

Early days

Luke's Gospel alone tells us how, at the age of 12 years, Jesus went with his parents to the Temple in Jerusalem for the Jewish festival of Passover. Mark begins his story with the baptism of Jesus in the River Jordan at the age of 30 years and the others also include this important event. It marked the beginning of the ministry of Jesus. It was also the moment when Jesus realised that he was God's Son.

After his baptism Jesus travelled through the northern part of Galilee talking to people about God. He chose twelve of his followers to be his disciples and he began to teach and train them. After Jesus left the earth eleven of these disciples (then called 'apostles') built up the Christian Church which is still with us today (see picture A).

A life's work

The message from God that Jesus gave to the people was simple. They should be deeply sorry for their sins (repent) and believe in God's good news. Jesus taught the people through stories (parables) which they found easy to remember. He also healed many people

B Christians celebrating Holy Communion. What are they remembering as they do this?

who were sick. Large crowds began to follow him believing that they were seeing God at work.

Others, though, opposed Jesus from the beginning. How could this man, whose parents were known to everyone, even dare to suggest that he was God? It was a serious crime for any Jew to make this claim. It was called 'blasphemy'.

The end and a new beginning

The last week in the life of Jesus began when he entered Jerusalem during the Passover festival. A few days later his last meal with his disciples was made memorable by the actions that he performed as he was giving them bread and wine. Ever since, Christians have remembered that meal, and the death of Jesus, each time they celebrate Holy Communion.

Later that night Jesus was betrayed to the Jewish authorities by one of his disciples, Judas Iscariot. A Jewish court, the Sanhedrin, tried and condemned him before he appeared in front of Pontius Pilate, the Roman governor. Condemned to death by Pilate, Jesus was soon executed. Three days later, Christians believe, he returned to life.

IN THE GLOSSARY
Apostle; Bethlehem; Blasphemy; Disciple; Gospel; Holy Communion; Jerusalem; Judas Iscariot; Luke; Matthew; Parable; Passover; Pontius Pilate; Temple.

WHAT DO YOU KNOW?

1 a How did Matthew and Luke begin their Gospels?

b How many followers did Jesus choose to be his disciples?

c What did Jesus tell the people?

d Why did large crowds of people follow Jesus?

e Why did it take Jesus' disciples a long time to realise just who he was?

2 Imagine that you are in the crowd following Jesus. Are you one of his followers or one of his critics? Explain your answer.

3 Jewish people believe very strongly that there is only one God. Why do you think that many of them found it very difficult to accept the teaching of Jesus?

The Life *of* Jesus

JOHN THE BAPTIST

- God sent John the Baptist to prepare the people for the coming of Jesus.
- John told his listeners that they needed to change their lives.
- Being baptised in the River Jordan was to be the sign that they wanted to change their way of life.

LOOK IN ▶ *Matthew 3.1–12*

John the Baptist, who appears at the beginning of all four Gospels, was an unusual character. Who was he? Why do each of the Gospels tell us about him? Why was he important in the life of Jesus?

I am the voice of one crying in the wilderness

The forerunner

John the Baptist was born around 7 BCE to Zechariah, a priest serving in the Temple in Jerusalem, and his wife, Elizabeth. The couple were elderly and childless. One day, in the Temple, Zechariah was told by an angel that he would father a special child. The child would be great in God's sight and filled with the Holy Spirit. He would prepare the people for the coming of Jesus by being his 'forerunner' – a person sent ahead of someone very important to tell the people about his arrival. Jewish leaders often sent a forerunner ahead of them.

John's message

John the Baptist was a holy man, or a prophet, who attracted large crowds into the desert to hear him preach. He was dressed in a rough camel-skin robe, tied around his waist by a leather belt. His daily diet was locusts (flying insects) and wild honey.

John told the people that if they had two shirts they must give one of them away. Tax collectors were told to take no more money from people than they were

A John was described as 'a voice crying in the wilderness'. What do you think this meant?

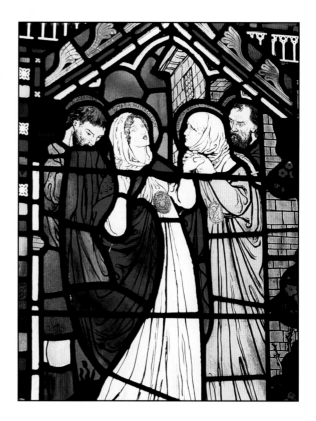

B Elizabeth visits Mary, the future mother of Jesus. We are told that Elizabeth's baby, John the Baptist, leapt in the womb of Elizabeth when the two women met. What was this intended to show?

allowed to collect. The Roman soldiers must not rob the people.

John and his baptism

Those who were sorry for their sins made their way to the River Jordan to be baptised by John. John 'dipped' them beneath the water to show that they had been cleansed from their sins by God. They could now make a new start since they were part of God's kingdom.

Most Christian Churches today baptise people to show that their sins have been forgiven. There are two different kinds of baptism:

a **Infant baptism**. Anglican, Roman Catholic and Orthodox Churches baptise babies by pouring water over their head.

b **Believer's baptism**. Baptist Churches baptise adult believers by immersing them beneath the water in the sea, a river or a pool in church.

The importance of John

All of the Gospels tell us that John told the people that someone far greater than himself was coming. It is not clear, however, whether John recognised Jesus to be that person. Certainly towards the end of his life, when he was in prison, John doubted whether Jesus was the promised Messiah.

IN THE GLOSSARY

Baptism; Believer's baptism; Gospels; Holy Spirit;
Infant baptism; John the Baptist; Messiah; Prophet.

WHAT DO YOU KNOW?

1 a Why was the birth of John the Baptist unusual?

b What part did John play in the early life of Jesus?

c What did John tell his listeners to do?

d How did John baptise people?

e What did the people receive through John's baptism?

2 Why do you think so many people wanted to travel into the desert to hear John the Baptist preaching?

3 What was the link between the lifestyle of John and his message to the people?

THE BIRTH OF JESUS

- Jesus was born in Bethlehem in 5 or 6 BCE.
- According to Matthew's Gospel the birth of Jesus was foretold to Joseph, whilst in Luke's Gospel the news was first given to Mary.
- In Luke's Gospel shepherds were the first visitors to the stable in Bethlehem whilst in Matthew's Gospel the Magi (Wise Men) were the first visitors.

LOOK IN ▶ *Matthew 1.18–2.12*
Luke 1.26–2.20

Centuries after the birth of Jesus monks tried to calculate when he was born. They were several years out in their calculations. We know that Herod the Great died in 4 BCE but he was alive when Jesus was born. Jesus was probably born in 5 or 6 BCE.

A Who was given the news that God's son, Jesus, was to be born?

The birth of Jesus

The birth of Jesus is recorded in the Gospels of Matthew and Luke. There are many differences between their accounts. Matthew tells us that the conception of Jesus was first announced by the angel to Joseph, his future father. This was a problem since Joseph and Mary, Jesus' mother, were not married although they had agreed to marry. Normally Joseph would have broken off the agreement. The angel, knowing this, told Joseph that the baby had been conceived by God's Holy Spirit.

In Luke's Gospel the birth of Jesus was announced to Mary and not Joseph. Mary was deeply worried by the news that she was to give birth to 'the Christ' (the Messiah). Jesus was God's Son. She was assured that God was the 'father' of her baby and not Joseph. Mary's song of praise to God after she received the news is called the Magnificat. It is still sung in many church services today.

The birth of Jesus took place in a stable in Bethlehem. The name of the child, Jesus, means 'God saves'.

B Why was the annoucement of the birth of Jesus to the shepherds important?

Visitors to the stable

In Luke's Gospel the first people to visit the baby were some poor shepherds. An angel had appeared to them whilst they were in a field near Bethlehem telling them that a special person had been born – and where he was to be found. Throughout Luke's Gospel it is the poor people, as here, who were most friendly towards Jesus.

Matthew does not mention the shepherds. He tells us that some 'Magi' (star-gazers) from the east visited Jesus. They brought gifts to the child – gold, frankincense and myrrh. Their visit was important for two reasons:

- the gifts were a reminder that the visitors saw Jesus as a king – although myrrh also looked forward to his death. Dead bodies were anointed with myrrh before they were buried.

- whilst the shepherds were Jewish visitors the Magi were not. They were Gentiles. This was to show that Jesus had come to help and heal everyone – Jews and Gentiles alike.

IN THE GLOSSARY

Bethlehem; Gentile; Gospels; Herod the Great; Holy Spirit; Joseph; Luke; Magi; Magnificat; Mary; Matthew; Messiah.

WHAT DO YOU KNOW?

1 a When was Jesus born?

b According to Matthew's Gospel, who first received the news that God's Son was to be born?

c In Luke's Gospel who was first told that Jesus was going to be born?

d What did the name 'Jesus' mean?

e Which gifts did the Magi bring to Jesus? What did they mean?

2 What do you think you would have done if you had been Joseph or Mary – and an angel had just told you that you were going to be the parent of God's Son?

3 Find out what Christians mean when they talk about the 'Virgin Birth'. Why do you think that some Christians believe that if God was born on earth then it would take a special kind of birth?

2 The Life *of* Jesus

JESUS GROWS UP

- Jesus was circumcised when he was eight days old to symbolise he was Jewish.
- Jesus was taught the Jewish Scriptures in the synagogue and at home.
- The parents of Jesus travelled to Jerusalem each year to celebrate the Passover festival in the Temple. Jews gathered from all over the Roman Empire.

LOOK IN ▷ *Matthew 2.13–23*

Jesus was born into an ordinary Jewish family. He was brought up by his parents, Mary and Joseph, in the northern Galilean village of Nazareth. He had lived there since he was a young child. From his earliest years he read the Jewish Scriptures, prayed with his parents in the local synagogue and celebrated all the Jewish festivals. They also taught him the Scriptures and Jewish prayers at home just as Jewish parents do today.

A *After Jesus' visit to the Temple in Jerusalem, when he was 12 years old, we hear no more of Joseph, his father. Why?*

Circumcision

Jewish parents circumcise all of their male children on the eighth day after they are born. In circumcision the foreskin on a boy's penis is removed to show that he belongs to the Jewish people. This custom originates from the time of Abraham who lived about 2,000 BCE. Abraham, the father of the Jewish nation, was told by God to circumcise all of the males in his large family – 318 people altogether – including himself! Jesus would probably have been circumcised in the Jerusalem Temple.

Every Jewish boy is still circumcised today. For centuries this ceremony was carried out by the father of the family. It was one of his most important responsibilities as a father. However, today it is usually performed by a mohel, a specially trained Jewish circumciser. It still takes place on the eighth day after a boy has been born, usually in his home.

B The Gospels show that Jesus had a normal upbringing. Why do you think it was important to stress this?

Jewish education

As far as we know Jesus was brought up just like any other Jewish boy. Jewish boys between the ages of five and thirteen were educated in their local synagogue by the rabbi or another religious leader. Learning the Jewish Scriptures off by heart was a very important part of this education and began as early as possible. The main purpose of going to school for a boy was to become a good Jew by learning and understanding the holy Scriptures.

Mary and Joseph would not have taken Jesus with them when they went to the magnificent Temple in Jerusalem, over 100 km away, each year for the great Passover festival. He would have stayed behind with older members of his family in the village. The Passover festival, still celebrated annually by Jews today, recalls the time around 1400 BCE when the Israelites were led from Egyptian slavery by God towards their Promised Land of Israel. There were many other Jewish festivals to be enjoyed each year but these were usually just celebrated in the village.

IN THE GLOSSARY

Abraham; Circumcision; Israel; Jerusalem; Joseph; Mary; Nazareth; Passover; Rabbi; Sabbath Day; Synagogue; Temple.

WHAT DO YOU KNOW?

1 a How old are Jewish boys when they are circumcised?

b Who was the first person to carry out circumcision? Why?

c Who is most likely to circumcise Jewish boys today?

d Where were Jewish boys educated in the time of Jesus? Who would have been their teacher?

e Which festival attracted most Jews to the Temple in Jerusalem?

2 What do you think each Jewish parent hoped for their child as they were growing up? How did they try to bring this about?

3 Circumcision is the oldest Jewish practice which is still carried out today. Why do you think Jewish parents have always considered it to be so important?

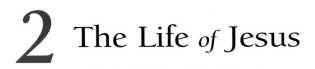

2 The Life *of* Jesus

IN THE TEMPLE

- The Passover was the most important Jewish festival.
- The bar mitzvah ceremony marked the moment when a Jewish boy was recognised as an adult.
- When Jesus stayed behind in the Temple he was showing that God's work must come first in his life.

LOOK IN ▶ *Luke 2.41–52*

The most important Jewish religious festival was, and still is, the Passover (Pesach). In the time of Jesus pilgrims, who were scattered all over the Roman Empire, travelled to Jerusalem. The parents of Jesus travelled to the holy city each year for the celebration. Until Jesus was 12 years old he stayed behind at home in Nazareth with his relatives.

Bar mitzvah

During the lifetime of Jesus a Jewish boy was regarded as an adult when he reached his twelfth birthday. He could play a part in worship in the synagogue and in the temple.

Today, a Jewish boy becomes an adult on his thirteenth birthday. This is marked by the service of bar mitzvah (son of commandment) in the local synagogue, held on the first Sabbath day after his birthday. During the service the boy reads a passage in Hebrew from the Jewish Scriptures (the Torah). His father tells him that he is now responsible for his own spiritual life before God, a responsibility which the father, until now, has carried for him.

In the Temple

The Temple in Jerusalem was a very important centre of Jewish worship in the first century. The first Temple had been built there by King Solomon almost a thousand years earlier but this had been destroyed by an invading army in 586 BCE. King Herod the Great

A Jesus helped his father in his carpenter's shop until he was 30 years old. How might this have helped him in his future work?

B The Temple in Jerusalem. When was this building finally destroyed?

had begun to rebuild the building but the finishing touches were not added until after Jesus died. Then it only stood for a few years before the Romans destroyed it brick by brick in 70 CE. It was never rebuilt again.

The Passover festival attracted very large crowds to the Temple and its outbuildings. When Jesus was 12 years old he was taken by his parents for the first time to celebrate the festival. After the festival Mary and Joseph set off home with their friends and relations. They thought that Jesus was with the party but soon found out that he had been left behind. They quickly returned to Jerusalem but it took them three days to find him.

They found him in the Temple. He was talking and arguing with the Jewish religious leaders. His parents began to tell him off because, by this time, they were very worried about him. Jesus told them that he had come to earth to do what God had asked and that he must get on with the job. His parents did not understand what he was talking about and they took him back home. We do not hear anything more about Jesus for the next 18 years.

IN THE GLOSSARY

Bar mitzvah; Jerusalem; Joseph; Mary; Passover; Sabbath Day; Synagogue; Temple; Torah.

WHAT DO YOU KNOW?

1 a Where did Mary and Joseph celebrate the Passover festival each year?
  b Who built the first and second Temples in Jerusalem?
  c Why did Jesus stay behind in the Temple in Jerusalem?
  d How did Jesus respond when his parents told him off?

2 Today in the Jewish community a boy is recognised as an adult at the age of 13 years. He becomes responsible for his own spiritual life. When do you think you will become a responsible adult?

3 What do you think Jesus was really telling his parents when he said that he had come to earth to do what God had asked? Why do you think they found this very difficult to understand?

BAPTISM AND TEMPTATIONS

- John the Baptist told the people to repent from their sins and be baptised by him in the River Jordan.
- Jesus was baptised by John. As Jesus left the water he heard God speaking to him from heaven.
- Jesus was tempted three times by Satan, the Devil, in the wilderness.

LOOK IN ▶ *Mark 1.9–11*
Matthew 4.1–11

Jesus was 30 years old when he made his first public appearance. He found John the Baptist who was busy preaching and

A How did God show that Jesus was his son at his baptism?

baptising people in the River Jordan. John was telling the people to turn away from their sins and show that they were sorry by being baptised.

Jesus is baptised by John

Jesus joined the crowd of people waiting to be baptised by John. After John had baptised him we are told that Jesus alone saw the heavens above him opening. God's Spirit was coming down on him just like a dove. A voice then spoke to Jesus out of heaven saying:

'You are my own dear Son. I am pleased with you.'

The voice that Jesus heard was that of God. Jesus was just about to begin his life's work. God was promising him that he would be with him at all times in the future.

Jesus is tempted

Following his baptism Jesus spent six weeks fasting on his own in the wilderness (desert). When people fast they go without food and water and spend time alone with God without any distractions. The Jews believed that the wilderness was the home of many

B Why was the baptism of Jesus immediately followed by the Devil's temptations?

evil spirits. They would never have spent any time alone there. It was far too frightening.

The Gospels tell us that Jesus was tempted by the Devil three times. The temptations took place as Jesus was trying to work out just what God wanted him to do with his future life.

- **Temptation one**   The Devil tempted Jesus to feed the many poor people around him by turning the stones of the desert into bread.

- **Temptation two**   Jesus was tempted to throw himself off the top of the Temple in Jerusalem. The

Devil reminded him that God could save him from hurting himself – and the people would be very impressed.

- **Temptation three**   Jesus was offered all the kingdoms of the world if he worshipped the Devil instead of God.

Jesus rejected each temptation by quoting verses from the Jewish Scriptures and the Devil left him alone for a while. Jesus was now free to get on with his life's work. The temptations show Jesus as someone who had the same doubts and weaknesses as everyone else but a person who was determined to live by God's law. In the end that determination cost him his life.

IN THE GLOSSARY
Devil; Gospels; Jerusalem; John the Baptist; Satan; Temple.

WHAT DO YOU KNOW?

1 a What was John the Baptist doing when Jesus found him?

b What was John telling the people to do?

c What was unusual about the baptism of Jesus?

d What did the Jews believe about the wilderness?

e What temptations were offered to Jesus?

2 Do you think the temptations happened just as they are recorded? Can you think of another possible way of understanding them?

3 Christians believe that Jesus was sinless. Yet, he came to John to be baptised and this included confessing his sins. If Jesus did not have any sins to be forgiven why should he want to be baptised?

THE DISCIPLES

- A disciple is a man or woman who follows the example and teachings of a great leader.
- Jesus chose twelve disciples, all men, to share his short public life with him.
- Peter, James and John belonged to an 'inner circle' of disciples. They were the closest friends of Jesus.

LOOK IN ▶ *Mark 1.16–28; 2.13–17*
Luke 6.12–16

A disciple is a pupil or a learner who follows the example and teachings of a teacher. Although Jesus had many

A Why were the disciples attracted to Jesus?

followers he chose twelve close friends or disciples who often called him 'rabbi' or 'teacher'. These people were later called 'apostles' rather than disciples when they were 'sent out' by Jesus to preach his message to the people. After the death of Jesus the apostles encouraged people to follow Jesus and become members of the Christian Church.

Choosing the disciples

The Gospels tell us about the ways in which some of the disciples followed Jesus. James, John, Peter and Andrew were all fishermen when Jesus called them to become disciples and leave their nets behind. Matthew was a much-hated tax collector, and working for the Romans, when he was invited to follow Jesus. Judas Iscariot was the disciple who later betrayed Jesus. There is very little information about the other disciples: Philip; Bartholomew; Thomas; James; Thaddaeus and Simon the Zealot.

The disciples soon discovered the cost of being a follower of Jesus. They left their home, family and careers to follow him. They had been warned of the cost. Jesus told them in very plain language:

B Jesus chose twelve friends from amongst his many followers for a particular reason. Why do you think he did this?

'None of you can be my disciple unless you give up everything you have.' (Luke 14.33)

The cost of being a disciple is made very clear in the Gospels. For example, read Mark 10.21–23 to find the answer Jesus gave to a young, rich man who wanted to become one of his followers. Jesus told him that he would have to give up all of his great wealth.

An inner circle

Three of the twelve disciples formed a kind of inner circle of close friends. Jesus took Peter, James and John with him when he needed their help and support. The three disciples accompanied Jesus on two occasions in particular:

• They were with Jesus when he was transfigured on a mountain in front of them.

• The three disciples were with Jesus on the night before he was crucified when he prayed desperately to God in the Garden of Gethsemane. Jesus needed their company but they were so tired they couldn't stay awake.

IN THE GLOSSARY
Andrew; Apostle; Disciple; Gospels; James; John; Judas Iscariot; Matthew; Peter; Rabbi.

WHAT DO YOU KNOW?

1 a What is a disciple?
b How many disciples did Jesus choose? What did they call Jesus?
c What were the disciples expected to do whilst Jesus was alive?
d Who belonged to the 'inner circle' of disciples?
e Which important occasions did this 'inner circle' share with Jesus?
2 The Gospels are full of occasions when the disciples failed Jesus. Why did they fail him so often? Why do you think we are told about these occasions?
3 Why did Jesus need a small group of disciples to share his deepest thoughts and experiences with?

2 The Life *of* Jesus

IN THE SYNAGOGUE

- The synagogue in Nazareth played a very important role in the education and religious life of Jesus as he grew up.
- Jesus returned to the synagogue later and read from the Scriptures on the Sabbath Day. This upset many people who then tried to kill him.
- Jesus found that he was not welcome in the synagogues of Palestine so he taught the people in the open-air.

LOOK IN ▶ *Luke 4.16–30*

As today, Jews in the time of Jesus met for worship in their local synagogue. The name itself means a place where people gather together. Jesus was brought up as a Jew and so the synagogue played a very important part in his life. He was taught in the local synagogue as a child. He would have worshipped there each Sabbath Day with his parents, brothers and sisters and celebrated all of the Jewish festivals in the synagogue. The Jews celebrate many festivals each year.

A What would you expect to find in the ark of a synagogue?

The synagogue

Jewish boys became adults on their twelfth birthday. Any Jewish man was allowed to read from the Scriptures on the Sabbath Day and explain what they meant. The Scriptures were written on scrolls and kept in a cupboard, called the ark, at one end of the synagogue. The scrolls of the Scriptures were highly treasured. The same still happens in Jewish synagogues today (see picture A).

Luke's Gospel tells us that it was the normal custom of Jesus to worship in the synagogue. Before Jesus became well-known he probably read from the Scriptures and explained them to the people many times. Mark's Gospel tells us of one occasion when Jesus was in Capernaum. The people who heard him teaching were amazed by what he said, and the way in

B *Who were allowed to read the Scriptures in a synagogue service?*

which he said it. Unlike the other teachers he spoke to them with great authority (Mark 1.21–22).

An incident in the synagogue

Jesus returned to Nazareth, the town in which he had been brought up. He went into the synagogue on the Sabbath Day. He read a passage from the Scriptures about someone who would come to bring God's good news to the poor and needy. He told the people that he was the one that God had promised to send to them.

The people were amazed by the way that Jesus spoke to them. Then Jesus suggested that he had come to help everyone, Jews and Gentiles. This greatly upset the people. It was not the message that they wanted to hear. They dragged Jesus out of the synagogue and took him to the top of the hill on which the town had been built. They intended to throw Jesus over the cliff. Somehow, though, Jesus managed to walk through the middle of the crowd unharmed and leave the city.

Since this incident Jesus stopped preaching in the synagogues. He began to preach in the open air instead. He probably did not feel welcome in the Jewish places of worship. Perhaps, too, the buildings were not large enough to house all the people who wanted to hear him.

IN THE GLOSSARY
Ark; Luke; Mark; Nazareth; Sabbath Day; Synagogue.

WHAT DO YOU KNOW?

1 a What were Jewish places of worship called?

 b What was it that amazed the people who heard Jesus teach in the synagogue in Capernaum?

 c What did Jesus read about in the synagogue in Nazareth?

 d How did the people react to the message of Jesus?

 e Why did Jesus begin to preach in the open air instead of the synagogue?

2 Imagine that you are listening to Jesus teaching in the synagogue. What do you think might have impressed you most?

3 Why do you think that the people reacted so strongly to the message that Jesus gave them in the synagogue in Nazareth?

2 The Life of Jesus

GOD'S KINGDOM

- In his teaching, especially his parables, Jesus wanted people to know that God's kingdom (rule) was growing on earth.
- In his kingdom God rules in the hearts and minds of people.
- God's kingdom grows on earth without people realising just what is happening.

LOOK IN ▶ *Matthew 18.1–4*
Mark 4.26–34

Jesus told many parables or short stories about God's kingdom. This kingdom was growing on earth even as he spoke. According to Mark's Gospel the first thing that Jesus told the people was:

> 'The right time has come and the kingdom of God is near! Turn away from your sins and believe the Good News!' (Mark 1.15)

A On more than one occasion Jesus welcomed little children. What lesson was he teaching about the kingdom of God by his actions?

The kingdom of God

When Jesus spoke about the kingdom of God he meant the rule of God on earth. In his kingdom God rules in the hearts and minds of those who follow and serve him. Jesus told two parables to explain how this kingdom is growing at the moment on earth:

a (Mark 4.26–29) In this parable Jesus explained that the kingdom of God was rather like a man scattering seed to the left and right on the ground. This was a familiar sight in Palestine. Once sown the man then forgot about the seed whilst it germinated beneath the earth's surface. The man does not understand how this happens – nor does he need to. Jesus, in his teaching, was sowing the seed but only God could make sure that the kingdom was growing unseen. Just as the seed grew beneath the surface of the earth so God's kingdom was growing without people realising what was happening around them.

b (Mark 4.30–34) In another parable Jesus explained that the kingdom of God was like a tiny grain of mustard seed. Once it has taken root in the earth it becomes a large plant. It grows so large, in fact, that birds of the air are able to build their nests in its strong branches. God's kingdom on earth is rather like

*B When Jesus placed a child in front of his disciples
he was acting out a parable. What lesson did
Jesus hope his disciples would learn?*

the tiny grain. It is much larger than people realise,
offering shelter to many people from far and wide.

Belonging to the kingdom

Jesus explained which kind of people could become
members of God's kingdom. In one conversation with
Jesus his disciples wondered who would be the
greatest in the new kingdom. To illustrate his answer
Jesus called to a child and placed him in front of the
disciples. He explained that the disciples must change,
and become like the child, before they could enter
God's kingdom. Jesus told them:

'The greatest in the Kingdom of heaven (God) is the
one who humbles himself and becomes like this
child.' (Matthew 18.4)

Anyone can enter God's kingdom if they have the
simple faith of a child. They do not have to be a Jew, a
religious person or even particularly good. They must
simply love God and love their neighbour as much as
they love themselves (John 13.34).

IN THE GLOSSARY
Disciple; Mark; Parable.

WHAT DO YOU KNOW?

1 a What did Jesus come to tell the people?

   b According to Mark's Gospel what were Jesus' first words?

   c Why is the kingdom of God like a man scattering seed on the earth?

   d How did Jesus answer his disciples when they asked who would be the greatest in
God's kingdom?

   e Who can enter God's kingdom?

2 Jesus said that anyone who wanted to enter God's kingdom must be like a child.
What childlike qualities do you think he had in mind?

3 In God's kingdom, God rules in the hearts and minds of people. What do you think
this means?

2 The Life *of* Jesus

THE BEATITUDES

- The Beatitudes contain the most important teachings of Jesus about the kingdom of God.
- The Beatitudes describe those people who are truly happy and sure of their place in the kingdom.
- The Beatitudes turn many of the values of this world upside down by describing the spiritual values that really matter.

LOOK IN ▶ *Matthew 5.3–12*

In Matthew's Gospel many of the teachings of Jesus are brought together (Chapters 5–7). Matthew presents them in the form of a sermon which Jesus gave on a mountain. Probably the teachings were given in many different places at different times.

The Sermon on the Mount changes the world's view as to what and who is important. In God's kingdom the person who is considered the least important in the eyes of society is the most important to God. Indeed it is only those who are unimportant in human eyes who can enter God's kingdom whilst others are left outside.

A Jesus teaching. Jesus said that the pure in heart will see God. Who do you think the pure in heart are?

The Beatitudes

The Beatitudes are written at the beginning of the Sermon on the Mount. In them Jesus describes what a person must do, or how they must behave, to be really happy. The Latin word 'beatus' means 'blessed' or 'happy'. Some of the sayings of Jesus in the Beatitudes take us by surprise because they are so unexpected. People listened to Jesus carefully because they had never heard anyone say the things that he said. He told them that:

a It is the poor in spirit who will inherit the kingdom of God. The people welcomed by Jesus were those who knew that they needed God because they were really poor.

B *Jesus said that the meek will inherit the earth. Who are the meek?*

b Those who mourn will be comforted by God. This includes those who have lost a loved one as well as those who are sad because of their sins.

c The meek will inherit the earth. The meek do not see themselves as important. Those who turned to Jesus for help – like the lepers and blind – found that God gave them all that they needed.

d Those who hunger and thirst for righteousness (for God) will have their needs fulfilled. Some of those who came to Jesus for help had to overcome obstacles first. This showed how serious they were.

e Those who forgive others will be forgiven by God.

f Those who are pure in heart will see God.

g Those who make peace between people will be called God's sons.

Finally, the Beatitudes end with a promise. Matthew wrote his Gospel around 80 CE. Many Christians, including some of the apostles, had already been persecuted. Some had even lost their lives because they were followers of Jesus. Jesus told them that anyone who was persecuted for his sake could be certain of a place in God's kingdom.

IN THE GLOSSARY

Apostle; Beatitudes; Gospels; Matthew; Sermon on the Mount.

WHAT DO YOU KNOW?

1 a What is the Sermon on the Mount?

b Who really matters in God's kingdom?

c What does the word 'Beatitude' mean?

d What did Jesus describe in the Beatitudes?

e Who did Jesus try to reassure at the end of the Beatitudes?

2 Imagine that you are reading the Beatitudes for the first time. Do you find any of them particularly surprising? Why?

3 The Beatitudes describe the kind of people that Jesus expected to be in God's kingdom. What do you think you can learn about God's kingdom by looking at the Beatitudes?

THE LORD'S PRAYER

- The Sermon on the Mount contains the most important teaching of Jesus about prayer.
- Jesus gave his followers 'a model prayer' to help them to pray.
- This prayer, the Lord's Prayer, is used in almost every Christian act of worship.

LOOK IN ▶ *Matthew 6.7–13*

The Sermon on the Mount contains the most important teaching of Jesus about prayer. Jesus often went away alone to pray, often onto a mountain or to a deserted place. He sometimes did this when he was being followed by crowds of people and was feeling tired. He wanted to encourage his followers to pray on their own as well. To do this Jesus gave

his disciples a 'model prayer' (the Lord's Prayer) for them to follow:

'Our Father in heaven' 'Abba', a word in the Aramaic language, really meant 'Daddy'. It was a very unusual word for Jesus to use. It encouraged his followers to think of their relationship with God as a very close one. Like all Jews Jesus believed that heaven was the home of God. It was also the place that all true believers would reach when they died.

'May your Kingdom come' Jesus believed that God's kingdom (rule) was going to be set up on earth. That kingdom was already growing just like a seed grows beneath the earth. In God's kingdom his will must be done – just as it is in heaven. God will rule in his own kingdom.

'Give us today the food we need' Jesus encouraged his followers to pray for their material needs to be met – but only day by day. Later, in the Sermon on the Mount, he told his followers not to worry about where their clothes, or food, will come from in the future (Matthew 6.25–34). If God looks after the tiny sparrow he will certainly look after them. The followers of Jesus were told to live their lives day by day.

A Is food the most basic human need?

Why do you think the Lord's Prayer is used frequently by all Christians, young and old?

of Job in which God allowed Satan (the Devil) to take away Job's health and family to test his faith. Jesus encouraged his followers to pray that they might be delivered from such temptation, and from the clutches of Satan himself.

The Lord's Prayer has been very important to Christians for centuries. It is included in almost every Christian act of worship. It is often used by individual believers in their prayers. They find a pattern in the Lord's Prayer on which to base the prayers that they address to God.

'Forgive us the wrongs we have done'   God is always waiting to forgive those who ask but there is a catch. God only forgives those who are prepared and ready to forgive others.

'Do not bring us to hard testing'   The people listening to Jesus would have known the Jewish Scriptures well. They would be familiar with the story

IN THE GLOSSARY
Aramaic; Devil; Disciple; Lord's Prayer; Satan; Sermon on the Mount.

WHAT DO YOU KNOW?

1 a Where do we find the most important teaching of Jesus about prayer?
b Why is the word 'Father' in the Lord's Prayer unusual?
c What does Jesus encourage his followers to pray about God's kingdom?
d Which people can expect God's forgiveness for their sins?
e Who was Satan and what did he do to Job?
2 Imagine that Jesus was giving his followers a model prayer today. What do you think the prayer might say?
3 Jesus encouraged his followers to pray only for the things they needed now. What do you think people need in order to live? Why do you think Jesus told them not to worry about the future? Is this realistic?

PARABLES (1)

- A parable is a story which carries a special moral or lesson for people to learn.
- Jesus told many parables and left his listeners to work out their meaning for themselves.
- The most well-known parable that Jesus told was that of the Good Samaritan.

LOOK IN ▶ *Luke 10.29–37*

People during the time of Jesus often listened to travelling story-tellers. Few of the stories they heard were written down and, in any case, most of the people could not read. Jesus was only one of many travelling preachers in Palestine during the first century who spread their message by telling stories.

A What made Jesus a good teacher?

Jesus and his parables

Jesus wanted to teach the people about God, and themselves, through the use of stories, or parables. A parable is a special story that carries a moral or a spiritual message. Usually Jesus told his story and left his listeners to work out what the message was. Many did not understand what his stories were saying. Jesus even suggested once that he told his stories to make the truth more difficult, not easier, to understand! His stories were often like puzzles and his listeners had to work hard to unravel their meaning. By working hard to understand them people showed that they were serious about entering God's kingdom.

The Good Samaritan

The parable of the Good Samaritan is probably the most well-known parable that Jesus told. It was told in answer to this question that Jesus was asked: 'Who is my neighbour?' Jesus responded by talking of a man who made the journey from Jerusalem to Jericho, a distance of some 30 km, on his own. The people listening to Jesus would have known the road well.

B How did the parable of the Good Samaritan challenge the prejudices of the listeners?

The ears of his Jewish listeners pricked up when Jesus told them that the man at the centre of his story was a Samaritan. The Jews and the Samaritans had been enemies for centuries. In the story a Jewish man is attacked, robbed and left for dead on the road. Two Jewish travellers passed by and left the man lying by the roadside. They probably thought that he was dead. It was a very serious thing for a Jew to touch a dead body. A third traveller, though, stopped, gave the man some first-aid and put him on his donkey. He took him to the nearest inn and paid for him to be looked after by the inn-keeper.

By now the listeners of Jesus were wondering why he told them the story and why a Samaritan was at the heart of it. Jesus did not make it easy for them. He left them to draw their own conclusions. In this way he forced them to face up to their own prejudices. In God's view Jews, Samaritans and everyone else were equally important. The parable of the Good Samaritan was his unforgettable way of putting this message across. His listeners found it almost impossible to believe that a Samaritan could do such a good thing, especially to a Jew!

IN THE GLOSSARY
Parable; Samaritan.

WHAT DO YOU KNOW?

1 a What is a parable?

b Why did Jesus often use parables to teach the people?

c In which part of Palestine was the story of the Good Samaritan set?

d Which question, asked by a lawyer, did Jesus answer by telling this parable?

e What lesson did Jesus want his listeners to take from the parable of the Good Samaritan?

2 Listening to a parable of Jesus has been likened to peeling an onion. What do you think this comment means?

3 Imagine you are a Jew standing in the crowd whilst Jesus is telling the parable of the Good Samaritan. What message do you think the parable might have for you?

PARABLES (2)

- **Jesus told three parables. Each describes an object, animal or a person being lost and found.**
- **The parables show God looking for the sinner who is lost.**
- **The parables show how happy God and the people are when they find that which was lost.**

LOOK IN ▷ *Luke 15.1–32*

Sometimes the writers of the Gospels collected the sayings and stories of Jesus and grouped them together because they had something in common. Luke's Gospel brings together three parables which had one thing in common – something or someone in the parable was lost and found.

A What lesson did Jesus want to teach through the story and why did he use a sheep as the subject?

a **The parable of the Lost Sheep.** You could see shepherds with their sheep everywhere in Palestine 2,000 years ago. Jesus often used common sights like this as the basis for his stories. In this story a shepherd is looking after 100 sheep and one of them becomes lost – as sheep often did. The good shepherd, when he discovers this, makes sure that the 99 other sheep are safe and then sets off to find the lost sheep. When he finds it he places it across his shoulders and then happily sets off for home. Once home he calls everyone together for a great feast.

b **The parable of the Lost Coin.** Most of the people living in Palestine were very poor. This explains why a woman who loses one of her ten silver coins sweeps the house from top to bottom to find it. She does not rest until she discovers where it is. When the coin is found she calls together all her friends and neighbours to share in her happiness.

c **The parable of the Lost Son.** This story is rather longer. A man had two sons. The younger one asked his father for his share of the inheritance which would come to him when his father died.

The father divided his estate between his two sons. Shortly afterwards, the younger son gathered all his possessions together and left home with his inheritance. Far from home he then squandered everything he had until nothing was left. A bad famine came and he had no money left to buy any food. He found a job feeding pigs and often ended up eating some of their food because he was so hungry.

Suddenly he had a bright idea. Why not return home and ask to become one of his father's servants? At least he would have regular meals. He set off only to discover that his father had been waiting and watching for him ever since he had left. His father met him on the road, gave him a new robe and shoes, and put a ring on his finger. That night his father arranged a special meal to which everyone was invited. The only person who did not come was his older brother. He could not see why his father was so happy to see his younger brother home.

The moral of the stories shows that God looks for that which has been lost, just like the woman and the shepherd. The parable of the lost son was not really about the two sons but about the father. Jesus wanted everyone to know that the father was really showing how God behaved all the time towards them. Even when people ignored him, or wasted what he had given them, God still welcomed them when they came home. The story may have been more complicated but the message was the same as that in the other two parables.

IN THE GLOSSARY
Gospels; Luke; Parable.

WHAT DO YOU KNOW?

1 a What did the shepherd discover when he counted his sheep?
  b Why did the woman sweep her house from top to bottom?
  c What did the younger son ask from his father?
  d What happened to the younger son?
  e What reception did the younger son receive from his father when he returned home?
2 We learn from the parable of the lost son that his older brother was not happy to see him return home and refused to join in the celebrations. Put yourself in the position of the older brother. What do you think your reaction might have been if your younger brother had returned home after wasting most of your father's money?
3 Each of these three stories ends with a great feast or banquet. What is the listener intended to learn from this?

2 The Life *of* Jesus

THE SABBATH DAY

- Jesus faced much opposition from the Pharisees and Sadducees.
- Often Jesus did not keep the strict laws about work on the Sabbath Day.
- By healing the man with the withered hand on the Sabbath Day Jesus was breaking the law.

LOOK IN ▶ *Matthew 12.1–14*

Jesus made both friends and enemies. Most of the opposition Jesus faced came from two religious groups, the Pharisees and the Sadducees. Jesus disagreed with them about how he and his disciples should keep the Sabbath Day, amongst other things.

A In recent years Sunday in this country has become like every other day of the week. Do you think this is a good idea?

The Sabbath Day

Jewish people have always rested from all work for one day a week – the Sabbath Day. This day begins at sunset on Friday evening and ends when three stars appear in the sky on Saturday night. When Jews celebrate this day they are following the example of God who created the world in six days and rested on the seventh after his work was finished.

Before the Sabbath Day starts all Jewish homes are cleaned and food is cooked. No cooking is done on the Sabbath Day. Everyone bathes and puts on their best clothes before the whole family sits down to eat a special meal together. Everyone goes to the synagogue on the Saturday morning where there are readings from the Holy Scriptures, the rabbi teaches and there are prayers. In the time of Jesus the Sabbath was a day of rest for all servants and animals as well. People could only take a 'Sabbath Day's journey' which was about 2,000 footsteps.

Jesus and the Sabbath Day

There were many times when Jesus, and his disciples, were accused of breaking the Sabbath Day laws. Here are two occasions:

a **The disciples of Jesus plucked corn on the Sabbath.** On one Sabbath Day Jesus walked through

B Do you treat Sunday like the other six days in the week?

a cornfield with his disciples. They began to pick a few ears of wheat and crush them in their hands. This upset the religious authorities who believed that the disciples were actually working and thus breaking the Sabbath laws. In reply Jesus told them something about himself. As God's Son Jesus was greater, and more important, than any of the religious laws. If he was not upset by what the disciples were doing then they shouldn't be either.

b **Healing a man with a withered arm.** Jesus entered a Jewish synagogue on the same day and saw a man with a shrivelled hand. The religious authorities asked Jesus whether it was alright to heal this man on the Sabbath Day. They knew that the Jewish law allowed a person's life to be saved on the holy day but this man's life was hardly in danger.

Jesus knew this. He also knew that if an animal fell into a pit on the Sabbath Day its owner was allowed to drag it out. If a person could do good for an animal on the Sabbath was the life of another human being not so much more valuable? He told the man to stretch out his hand and it was healed. His enemies were very upset and they began to plot to kill him.

IN THE GLOSSARY

Disciple; Pharisee; Rabbi; Sabbath Day; Sadducee; Synagogue.

WHAT DO YOU KNOW?

1 a When does the Sabbath Day begin and end?

b Why do Jews keep the Sabbath as a day of complete rest?

c What was a 'Sabbath Day's journey'?

d How did the disciples of Jesus break the Sabbath Day laws by crushing corn?

e Why was Jesus criticised for healing the man with the withered hand on the Sabbath Day?

2 Can you think of two advantages of having a day of complete rest once a week?

3 Why do you think Jesus was not very concerned about keeping the Sabbath Day laws?

2 The Life *of* Jesus

THE OUTSIDERS

- Many of those who followed or responded to Jesus were 'outsiders' and rejected by others.
- Lepers were outsiders. Jesus healed 10 lepers on one occasion yet only one, a Samaritan, returned to thank him.
- Tax collectors were outsiders because they worked for the Romans. Zacchaeus, a tax collector, promised to repay all the people he had cheated after he met Jesus.

LOOK IN ▶ *Luke 17.11–19*
Luke 19.1–10

Jesus was not against the religious leaders of his time. He simply found that they did not respond to what he said and did. However, there were many others who did. Most of these people were 'outsiders'. Amongst the outsiders who listened to Jesus were lepers and tax collectors. No one, except Jesus, wanted to have anything to do with them.

A Was it simply fear that made people treat lepers so badly?

a Healing ten lepers. It was a miserable life being a leper in Palestine. In the Gospels leprosy was called a 'dreaded skin disease'. As soon as a person was seen to have the disease they were banished to a home outside the village. They were only allowed to have contact with other lepers. If a leper came into the town he had to wear torn clothes, cover his mouth and shout 'unclean' wherever he went. Everyone made sure that they kept their distance as he, or she, passed.

No one would dream of talking with a leper or touching one. Leprosy was thought to be a highly contagious disease. On one occasion Jesus came across 10 lepers who shouted out to him from a distance, 'Jesus, Master, have pity on us'. Jesus did and healed them. One of them returned to thank Jesus and threw himself at his feet as a mark of respect. This man was from Samaria – a nation hated by all Jews. He was already healed but Jesus told him that his faith had made him well. This outsider went away a very happy man.

b Zacchaeus – the tax collector. Tax collectors were the

B Why was Zacchaeus such an outsider?

most hated of people in Palestine. They worked for the Romans and collected taxes from the Jews. They usually became very wealthy since they charged the people extra taxes. Jesus had already chosen one tax collector – Matthew – to be a disciple.

Now Jesus came across another, Zacchaeus. As if being a tax collector was not bad enough, Zacchaeus was so small that he couldn't see Jesus over the top of the crowd. He climbed a sycamore tree just outside the city of Jericho and when Jesus passed by he spotted Zacchaeus. He stopped and told the tax collector that he would like to visit his house.

This was a very unusual thing for Jesus to do. Rabbis didn't talk to tax collectors or lepers. They certainly did not visit the homes of those whom everyone else saw as traitors. The disciples of Jesus were not at all happy. Jesus, though, knew that Zacchaeus needed his help. The tax collector promised to pay back four times the amount of money he had taken from people illegally. He also said that he would give away half of his possessions to the poor. In return Jesus told Zacchaeus that he and his family would be saved.

IN THE GLOSSARY

Disciple; Gospels; Matthew; Palestine; Rabbi; Samaritan.

WHAT DO YOU KNOW?

1 a How were lepers treated during the life of Jesus?

   b What did Jesus do when 10 lepers shouted to him from a distance?

   c Why was the reaction of just one of the lepers important?

   d Why were tax collectors hated by all Jews?

   e What did Jesus tell Zacchaeus and how did Zacchaeus react?

2 Jesus told Zacchaeus that he and his family would be 'saved'. What did Jesus mean?

3 Can you think of two groups of people who are treated as outsiders or outcasts in our community? What makes them outsiders? What do you think the reaction of Jesus would have been towards them?

MIRACLES (1)

- The Gospels tell us that Jesus performed many miracles.
- Jesus healed a paralysed man and brought a young girl back to life.
- Jesus often taught people to keep quiet about his miracles. He did not want people to follow him just because of them.

 **LOOK IN** *Matthew 9.18,19*
Mark 2.1–12

In the Gospels we are told that Jesus healed many people in need – the blind, the sick, the deaf and dumb, the crippled and those possessed by evil spirits. He brought three dead people back to life – a boy, a girl and a friend, Lazarus. Jesus also calmed a storm at sea; turned water into wine; walked on water and told his disciples where to catch enough fish to break their nets.

A wonder-worker?

Josephus was a Jewish writer who lived around the time of Jesus. He described Jesus as a 'wonder-worker'. This is partly true. The Gospels certainly describe him doing things that the people at the time thought were miracles. Jesus, though, did not want people to follow him simply because he had extraordinary powers.

There were many other people at the time who were also wonder-workers. Some of them had followers (disciples) of their own. In contrast to them Jesus tried to keep many of the things he did secret. Often, after healing someone, he told them not to tell anyone else about what had happened.

Two miracles

Here are two healing miracles that Jesus performed:

a **Healing Jairus' daughter**. In picture A Jesus can be seen visiting the house of Jairus, an important Jewish leader. Jairus' daughter had just died and he came to

A Why did Jesus not want anyone, outside the family, to know what he had done for the little girl?

B Why were the religious leaders upset by what Jesus said to the paralysed man lowered down through the roof?

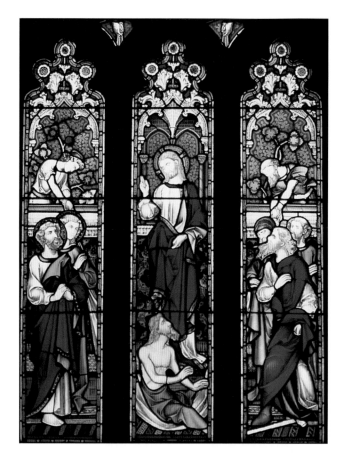

Jesus hoping that he could bring her back to life. Jesus took the little girl by the hand and told her to get up. She got to her feet immediately and everyone in the house was amazed. Jesus gave strict instructions to the family not to tell anyone about the miracle.

b **Healing a paralysed man**. On another occasion (picture B) a man, who had been paralysed for a long time, was carried by four friends on a stretcher to the house in which Jesus was teaching. There were too many people in the house for them to reach Jesus so they carried their friend onto the roof, unrolled the straw and let him down at the feet of Jesus.

Jesus upset the religious leaders by telling the man that his sins had been forgiven. They strongly believed that only God could forgive a person's sins. They knew immediately that Jesus was claiming to be God by what he was saying. Jesus forgave the man's sins. He also told him to rise up, pick up his bed and walk home. The man did just that.

IN THE GLOSSARY
Blasphemy; Gospels; Miracle; Palestine.

WHAT DO YOU KNOW?

1 a Name three kinds of miracle that Jesus performed.

 b How did Josephus describe Jesus?

 c Who was Jairus?

 d What did Jesus tell Jairus and his family after bringing the little girl back to life?

 e How did the paralysed man reach Jesus?

2 When Jesus was criticised for telling the man that his sins were forgiven he asked the religious leaders which was the easier thing to do – to tell the man that his sins were forgiven or to heal him. Imagine that you are one of the religious leaders. How would you answer this question of Jesus?

3 For Jewish people living in the time of Jesus the greatest sin that anyone could commit was to claim to be God's equal – or God himself. The sin was called 'blasphemy'. Why do you think Jewish people took this so seriously?

2 The Life *of* Jesus

MIRACLES (2)

- Jesus performed many miracles which demonstrated his power, as God's Son, over nature.

- The most important 'nature-miracle' describes how he fed a large crowd of people with two small fish and five loaves of bread.

- By calming a raging sea Jesus was claiming to have the same power as God.

LOOK IN  *Matthew 14.15–21*
Mark 4.37–41

Apart from healing people Jesus also performed other kinds of miracles. In one miracle he fed a large crowd which had followed him into the desert. This miracle, the feeding 5,000 people, was the most important that Jesus performed. Other miracles showed his authority over nature. He walked, for example, on water and calmed a very stormy sea.

a Jesus fed 5,000 people. This story, above all others, supports the belief of early Christians that Jesus had extraordinary power over ordinary things in life. This particular miracle was thought to be so important that it can be found in the Gospels six times, although in two accounts Jesus is said to have fed only 4,000 people. In the story Jesus fed a large crowd of people, using just five loaves and two small fish provided by a young boy.

To understand the importance of this miracle you must understand two pieces of background information:

- The ancestors of the hungry people had left slavery in Egypt about 1300 years earlier and had travelled across the desert in search of their Promised Land. On the journey they had been fed miraculously by God who provided manna from heaven each morning for them to eat. Now Jesus was feeding them, equally miraculously, in the desert.

A Which event would the feeding of the 5,000 remind the people of?

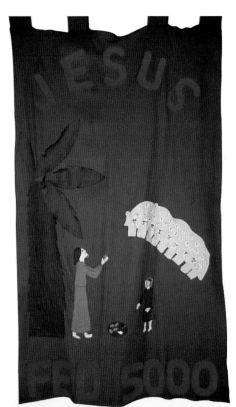

B The disciples were experienced fishermen. Why do you think they were so frightened by the storm on the lake?

- The most important act of worship in the early Church, as in the Christian Church today, was Holy Communion. At this service Christians remember the death of Jesus on the cross. Christians have always believed that God feeds them spiritually each time they share Holy Communion with each other.

b **Jesus calming a storm**. Jesus sailed across the Sea of Galilee with his disciples. This inland lake was renowned for its sudden storms. When the storm blew up the disciples were upset that Jesus was sleeping in the stern of the boat showing no concern for their safety. They woke him up, frightened for their lives. Jesus ordered the winds and the waves to subside. Jesus then wondered where the faith of the disciples was. The disciples were terrified and asked each other:

'Who is this? Even the wind and the waves obey him.'

The answer of the early Christians to this question was obvious. Jesus was no ordinary person. They believed him to be God's Son.

IN THE GLOSSARY
Disciple; Gospels; Holy Communion; Miracle.

WHAT DO YOU KNOW?

1 a Name two miracles that Jesus performed other than healing miracles.
   b Which miracle is recorded in the Gospels six times?
   c Which Christian act of worship was inspired by the feeding of the 5,000?
   d What do Christians remember at Holy Communion?
2 Some people believe that the nature-miracles of Jesus are not as important as the healing-miracles. Do you agree?
3 The early Christians believed that it was very important to show that Jesus was God. Why do you think this was so important to them?

PICTURES OF JESUS

- Jesus often spoke about God. When he called God his 'Father' he upset many people.
- In John's Gospel Jesus used seven 'word pictures' to describe himself.
- For many of these sayings Jesus took his 'pictures' from everyday life.

Jesus often spoke of his own relationship with God. It was very special to him. He described God as his 'Father' and spoke of himself as God's 'Son'. To explain his relationship with God Jesus said:

'My Father has given me all things. No one knows the Son except the Father, and no one knows the Father except the Son and those to whom the Son chooses to reveal him.' (Matthew 11.27)

A Why did Jesus paint 'word pictures' to help people to understand more about him?

Pictures of Jesus

In John's Gospel there are seven 'word pictures' given by Jesus which help us to understand a little bit more about him. Each word picture begins with the words 'I am':

a '**I am the bread of life.** Those who come to me will never be hungry; those who believe in me will never be thirsty.' (John 6.35)

   Everyone needs to eat and drink to stay alive and healthy. Jesus promised to spiritually feed through his teaching those who came to him and became his followers.

b '**I am the light of the world.** Whoever follows me will have the light of life and will never walk in darkness.' (John 8.12)

   Jesus brought light wherever he went. He told the people about God and removed darkness by performing miracles and helping those in need.

c '**I am the gate for the sheep…** Whoever comes in by me will be saved…' (John 10.7,9)

   More than once Jesus spoke of humans as being like sheep. Each night sheep were locked away in a pen to keep them safe. Jesus promised to keep those who followed him safe.

d '**I am the good shepherd,** who is willing to die for the sheep.' (John 10.11)

B What was Jesus trying to say about himself when he called himself the 'Good Shepherd'?

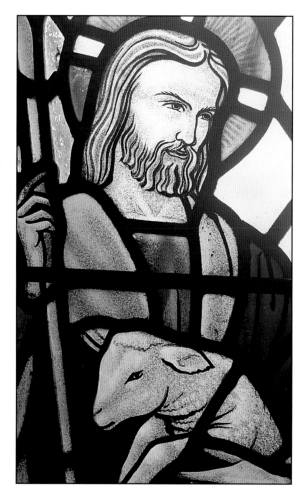

The shepherd protected his sheep at all costs. Often he placed his life at great risk by putting himself between his sheep and wild animals that threatened them. Soon Jesus was to die for his followers.

e **'I am the resurrection and the life.** Those who believe in me will live, even though they die…' (John 11.25)

Three days after being put to death Jesus rose again. He promised all of his followers that they, too, would rise from death.

f **'I am the way, the truth and the life;** no one goes to the Father except by me.' (John 14.6)

Jesus showed people the way to God. Others claimed to to do this but Jesus alone was God's Son.

g **'I am the real vine, and my Father is the gardener.'** (John 15.1)

Jesus had come to show people the way to God's kingdom. All those who belonged to that kingdom were like parts of a vine. They were a part of Jesus and God himself looked after his kingdom to make sure it grew properly.

IN THE GLOSSARY
Gospels; John.

WHAT DO YOU KNOW?

1 a What word did Jesus often use to describe God?

b What does the good shepherd do?

c What did Jesus do for his followers?

d What did Jesus promise his followers after death?

2 Jesus called himself the 'Good Shepherd' (see picture B). This picture was intended to help his followers understand a little more about him. What do you think they took from this picture of Jesus?

3 Jesus called God his Father and he encouraged his followers to do the same. Why do you think Christians today might find it helpful to think of God as their Father in heaven? Can you think of any ways in which this image might not be helpful?

2 The Life of Jesus

PRAYER

- Jesus taught his disciples the 'Lord's Prayer' when they asked him to teach them how to pray.
- Jesus set others an example by spending much time praying to God.
- Jesus taught that people should continue to pray even when their prayers are not being answered.

LOOK IN ▸ *Luke 11.5–8*

Jesus was born into a Jewish family. Like every other Jewish child he was taught the traditional Jewish prayers. Every morning and evening he would have said the most important Jewish prayer – the Shema:

A What do you think praying is?

'The Lord – and the Lord alone – is our God. Love the Lord your God with all your heart, with all your soul, and with all your strength.' (Deuteronomy 6.4–5)

The Shema expresses the Jewish belief that there is only one God. Christians and Jews share this belief.

Jesus and prayer

There are many times in the Gospels when Jesus went away on his own to pray. It often happened after he had spent a busy time preaching and healing. Sometimes Jesus found a hill, or a mountain, on which he could spend time on his own praying to God. He also prayed if he had a great decision to make or something frightening to face. For example, he prayed before he chose his twelve disciples and in the Garden of Gethsemane before he was arrested towards the end of his life.

One day the disciples found him praying on his own and asked him to teach them how to pray. Jesus taught them the prayer which is known as the Lord's Prayer. This prayer is used by Christians today in most of their services:

B Apart from asking God for things, are there other reasons for praying?

'Our Father in heaven, May your holy name be honoured; may your Kingdom come; may your will be done on earth as it is in heaven. Give us today the food we need. Forgive us the wrongs we have done as we forgive the wrongs that others have done to us. Do not bring us to hard testing, but keep us safe from the Evil One.' (Matthew 6.9–13)

Advice about prayer

Jesus taught his followers that prayer is all about talking to their Father (God) in heaven. He criticised those religious leaders who made it difficult for other people to pray.

In one parable that Jesus told about prayer a traveller arrives unexpectedly at a friend's house at midnight. The friend goes to a neighbour to ask for some food but his neighbour refuses to help. However, the person will not go away and eventually his neighbour gives in because he is so persistent. Jesus told the story to illustrate the truth that his followers should always pray and never be discouraged.

IN THE GLOSSARY
Disciple; Gospels; Lord's Prayer; Shema.

WHAT DO YOU KNOW?

1 a What is the name of the most important Jewish prayer?

b Which prayer do Christians use in most of their services?

c What name did Jesus give to God?

d List two things that Jesus taught his disciples about prayer.

e Why does God answer prayer, according to Jesus?

2 Read Matthew 6.5–7. Why do you think Jesus was critical of those who prayed where others could see them? Why do you think anyone would want to do that anyway?

3 Why do you think Jesus, God's Son, found it necessary to pray before making an important decision, or before facing a difficult situation?

2 The Life *of* Jesus

CAESAREA PHILIPPI

- Jesus wanted to know from his disciples what the people thought of him.
- Jesus also asked his disciples what they thought of him and Simon, speaking for them, replied that he was God's Messiah.
- This answer pleased Jesus who gave Simon the name 'Peter', meaning a 'rock'.

LOOK IN ▶ *Matthew 16.13–20*

Usually when we come across the disciples in the Gospels they have misunderstood what Jesus was saying or doing. Occasionally, however, the truth seems to have dawned on them. One incident which took place at the small town of Caesarea Philippi shows this very well.

A Why did some people believe Jesus was John the Baptist brought back to life?

The opinions of the people

Jesus was alone with his disciples. He wanted to know what the people, and the disciples, thought of him. The disciples told him that some people thought that he was John the Baptist brought back to life. John, the cousin of Jesus, had recently been put to death by Herod the Great.

Others believed that he was Elijah, a great Jewish prophet. Jews believed that Elijah would return to the earth before their promised leader, the Messiah, came. Every year, in their great Passover festival, they set a place for Elijah in case he came back during the festival. Others thought that Jesus was Jeremiah, another great Jewish prophet.

The opinion of Peter

Jesus turned to his disciples and asked for their personal opinion. Simon, so often the spokesman for the group, spoke up. He said to Jesus:

'You are the Messiah.'

The Messiah was the leader that the Jews expected God to send to deliver them from their enemies. Jesus knew himself to be that Messiah but he was going to be rather different to the person who the Jews were

B Why did Peter's statement please Jesus so much?

expecting. They were looking for a warrior-king who would throw the Romans out of Palestine and set the Jews free. Jesus, though, was going to be a suffering leader who would die on a Roman cross and rise from the dead three days later. No wonder few people recognised him as the Messiah.

Here, though, Simon was the exception. Jesus was delighted when Simon spoke. He had seen the truth. Jesus told Simon that he could not have discovered this truth unless God himself had made it known to him. To underline the importance of what Simon had said Jesus gave him a new name. From now on he would be called the 'rock' (Peter) who would become the foundation on which the Christian Church would be built.

Christians have long disagreed amongst themselves about the importance of these words. To Roman Catholics, who believe that Peter became the first Bishop of Rome (Pope), this is one of the most important statements in the Gospels. Jesus gave to Peter the keys of heaven and hell. He then ordered the disciples not to tell anyone that he was the Messiah. Jesus knew that if they did then the people would only get the wrong idea about him.

IN THE GLOSSARY

Disciple; Gospels; Herod the Great; John the Baptist; Messiah; Palestine; Passover; Peter; Prophet; Protestant; Roman Catholic Church.

WHAT DO YOU KNOW?

1 a Which three people did many of the people of Palestine believe Jesus to be?

b Why was a place set for Elijah at the Passover meal?

c Who was the Messiah?

d Why was Jesus a different kind of Messiah from the one who the Jews were expecting?

e What do Roman Catholics believe happened to Peter?

2 Imagine yourself to have been a Jew living in Palestine in the time of Jesus. Why might you have found Jesus to be a great disappointment?

3 Jesus knew himself to be God's Messiah but did not want the people to know. Why?

THE TRANSFIGURATION

- Jesus was 'transfigured' in front of three of his disciples on a mountain-top.
- During this extraordinary event Moses and Elijah appeared to Jesus.
- After Jesus was transfigured he told his disciples to say nothing about what they had seen until after he had risen from the dead.

LOOK IN ▶ *Mark 9.2–13*

There are some events in the life of Jesus, like the Transfiguration, which are very difficult to understand. On this occasion Jesus was 'transfigured' (his appearance was changed) in front of three disciples

A Why were mountains thought to be the most likely places for God to appear?

on a mountain. We do not know whether this actually happened or whether it was a vision.

A cloud and a mountain

God is said to have 'spoken' to several people in the Old Testament and many of these meetings took place on mountains. People believed that the higher they climbed up a mountain the closer they came to heaven – the place where God lived. The Jews thought that God was so holy that if someone saw him they would die. Not even the holiest people in the Old Testament could speak with God face to face. For this reason a cloud always came down as God met with them.

Jesus on the mountain

On this occasion Jesus went with his three closest friends (Peter, James and John) to the top of a mountain. He wanted to spend some time quietly praying with them. When the four of them reached the top the appearance of Jesus was totally changed and his clothes became a shining, dazzling white. The disciples saw for a brief moment Jesus as he really was – the Son of God. Two of the most important people in the Old Testament then appeared to him:

- **Moses**. Moses received the Ten Commandments from God and passed them on to the Israelites.

B What was celebrated during the Feast of Tabernacles?

- **Elijah**. Elijah was the first great prophet in Jewish history. The Jews believed that Elijah would return to earth before the Messiah came. Jesus believed that he was God's Messiah.

The disciples were scared by what they saw. Peter broke the silence by offering to build shelters (tabernacles) for Jesus, Moses and Elijah to live in. Each year, at the Feast of Tabernacles, Jews have always built shelters to remind them of the time that their ancestors travelled across the desert for years without a permanent home. At that moment the cloud covered them all and God spoke:

'This is my own dear Son – listen to him!' (Mark 9.7)

Jesus had heard the same words when he was baptised.

On the way down the mountain Jesus told his disciples to say nothing about what they had seen until he had risen from the dead. Since this incident Jesus talked more openly to them about his coming death in Jerusalem. The more openly he spoke, though, the less they understood.

IN THE GLOSSARY

Disciple; Elijah; James; Jerusalem; John; Messiah; Moses; Old Testament; Peter; Ten Commandments.

WHAT DO YOU KNOW?

1 a Which three friends shared the experience of the transfiguration with Jesus?

b Which two characters from the Old Testament appeared to Jesus on the mountain?

c What was the cloud that fell on the mountain demonstrating?

d Which festival did Peter initiate by offering to build tabernacles for Jesus, Moses and Elijah?

2 Why do you think Peter acted the way he did? How do you think you might have acted if you had been present?

3 Are you inclined to believe that the transfiguration was an actual event which took place or a vision that people saw in their minds? Do you think it matters either way?

2 The Life *of* Jesus

CONFLICT

- The religious leaders opposed Jesus from the beginning of his ministry.
- They heavily criticised Jesus for mixing with 'outsiders'.
- Jesus criticised the many rules about keeping the Sabbath Day.

 **LOOK IN** *Mark 2.13–17*
Luke 19.45–48

Wherever Jesus went large crowds followed to listen to what he had to say and to see the miracles he performed. Yet Jesus was not everyone's favourite religious teacher. Many people felt threatened by what he had to say.

A Why did the religious leaders find Jesus to be such a threat?

Conflict and opposition

The Gospels suggest that the opposition to Jesus from the religious leaders was there from the beginning. For example, the first time Mark's Gospel mentions the enemies of Jesus he was at a party with his friends. Jesus obviously enjoyed celebrating with others because he performed his first miracle at a wedding-feast when the wine ran out (John 2.1–10). His wide circle of friends earned him the reputation amongst his enemies of being 'a glutton and a drinker, a friend of tax collectors and other outcasts!' (Matthew 11.19)

The company that Jesus kept brought him much criticism. So, too, did his attitude towards the religious leaders of the time – the Pharisees, Sadducees and scribes. There is no doubt that many well-meaning people in this group were uncomfortable with some of the things that Jesus said and did. The Jews believed it was their responsibility to look after the Sabbath. Jesus agreed with them that there was something special about this day. He felt uncomfortable, however, with many of the rules and laws that the people had to keep on the Sabbath. In particular, Jesus always insisted that people, and their needs, were much more important than the Sabbath Day laws and not the other way round.

B The Romans were very reluctant to be drawn into the conflict between Jesus and the religious leaders. Why?

Jesus, the teacher

Jesus left the people with a whole series of sayings that they could remember. His teaching was simple and direct, appealing to the people's imagination. He told them stories about fields of grain; lost coins; lost sheep; lost sons and other every day topics. They could understand Jesus when he spoke to them about God and the kingdom which he was building on earth. The people had waited a long time for God to send his Messiah to them and when he began to speak of God as a father and a king they understood what he was talking about. More than once a comparison was drawn between the teaching of Jesus and that of the religious leaders.

A final falling out

By the time he arrived in Jerusalem for the Passover festival towards the end of his life there was open warfare between Jesus and the religious leaders. One of the first things Jesus did on arriving was to go into the Temple and overthrow the tables of the people selling there. Since these people had paid the religious authorities to be there Jesus was openly challenging the leaders to do their worst. Within a few hours Jesus received their answer.

IN THE GLOSSARY

Disciple; Gospels; Jerusalem; Mark; Messiah; Passover; Pharisee; Sabbath Day; Sadducee; Scribe; Temple.

WHAT DO YOU KNOW?

1 a Where did the main opposition to Jesus and his message come from?

b Which three religious groups made up the opposition?

c Describe Jesus' first miracle?

d What did Jesus say about the Sabbath Day?

e Compare Jesus' teaching with that of the religious leaders?

2 Why did Jesus upset the religious leaders by mixing with the outsiders?

3 If Jesus was on earth today do you think he would meet with stiff opposition? Who do you think would oppose Jesus?

Death *and* beyond

ENTERING JERUSALEM

- Jesus took a great risk by entering Jerusalem just before the Passover festival.
- Jesus entered the city on a donkey and was welcomed by a large crowd.
- Christians remember this event every year on Palm Sunday.

LOOK IN ▷ *Mark 11.1–25*

A few days before he was crucified Jesus arrived in Jerusalem with his disciples. It was spring and the city was filling up with Jewish pilgrims arriving for the great Passover festival. This festival reminds Jews of the time, hundreds of years earlier, when God delivered their ancestors from slavery in Egypt. When Jesus arrived in Jerusalem it was crowded and not everyone could find lodgings in the city itself. Jesus stayed with some friends in nearby Bethany.

Entering the city

Jesus knew that he was taking a great risk entering Jerusalem. The Roman soldiers would have arrested him if they had known that he was claiming to be the Messiah. The Messiah would have been seen as a great threat to the power of Caesar. Many of the Pharisees, Sadducees and other Jewish leaders lived in the city. They had already expressed their opposition to this wandering preacher from Galilee many times. They were upset that Jesus broke the religious laws and mixed with undesirable people like tax collectors and prostitutes. Jerusalem was the best place for them to put a stop to Jesus – they had most influence there.

Jesus walked about 130 km from Galilee to Jerusalem. He entered the city in a surprising way – on a donkey. The city went wild with excitement. The people laid their coats on the road and ripped down palm branches. Jesus was fulfilling a prophecy from the Old Testament prophet, Zechariah. He had said:

A Is this a good way of making the Bible come alive for people?

B Why are these people waving palm crosses as they walk along?

'Tell the city of Zion (Jerusalem), Look, your king is coming to you! He is humble and rides on a donkey…' (Matthew 21.5)

The people in the city would have known this quotation well. The donkey was an animal of peace whereas a horse was an animal of war. Jesus was offering God's peace to the people of Jerusalem.

At the same time Jesus was also making a claim on the people – he wanted to be their king. This king was setting up a spiritual kingdom on earth. It was already well underway. The disciples were aware of what Jesus was doing. They joined with the crowd in shouting out their welcome to him.

Palm Sunday

The entry of Jesus into Jerusalem marked the beginning of the last week of his human life. After this happened events were to move quickly towards his death on a cross. Christians today recognise the importance of this event. Each year many churches re-enact Jesus riding on the donkey into Jerusalem (see pictures A and B). They hold processions through their local towns or villages carrying palm leaves or crosses with them through the streets. Palm crosses link together Palm Sunday and Good Friday (the day on which Jesus died). Palm Sunday marks the beginning of Holy Week, the most serious time in the year for Christians, which ends with Easter Saturday. On the following day, Easter Sunday, Christians celebrate the rising of Jesus from the dead.

IN THE GLOSSARY
Disciple; Easter Sunday; Good Friday; Jerusalem; Messiah; Palm Sunday; Passover; Pharisee; Sadducee.

WHAT DO YOU KNOW?

1 a What did Jews remember each year during the Passover festival?

b Why might the Romans have arrested Jesus?

c How did Jesus enter Jerusalem?

d When do Christians especially remember the entry of Jesus into Jerusalem on a donkey?

e What kind of king did Jesus want to be?

2 Imagine that you had been one of the crowd in Jerusalem. Would you have been among those welcoming Jesus as your king?

3 The very people who welcomed Jesus into Jerusalem on the Sunday were demanding his death on the Thursday. Does this surprise you?

3 Death *and* beyond

THE LAST SUPPER

- Judas Iscariot, one of the disciples, agreed to betray Jesus to the religious authorities.
- Jesus ate a final meal with his disciples on the first night of the Passover festival.
- Christians keep alive their memories of the death of Jesus by celebrating Holy Communion.

LOOK IN ▶ *Mark 14.12–26*

Judas, one of the disciples of Jesus, changed sides. We do not know why. He may have become disillusioned with Jesus. Maybe he had hoped that Jesus would be a warrior-leader who would lead the Jews against the Romans. There may have been some other reason. Whatever his reason, Judas offered to betray Jesus to the religious authorities for 30 pieces of silver – a year's wage for a labourer.

A Why did Jesus want to share his last Passover meal with his disciples?

Disturbing news

The Passover festival had begun. On the first night Jesus met with his disciples to have a special meal (picture A). The Passover always begins in this way. Every Jew has a special meal with members of his or her own family. The disciples were the 'family' of Jesus.

Jesus arranged for them to eat together in a room in a house owned by a friend. Whilst they were eating Jesus told them the disturbing news that one of them was going to betray him to the religious authorities. They were even more disturbed when Jesus told them that they would all shortly desert him when he needed them most.

The last meal

Jesus took a piece of bread, thanked God, broke it and distributed it amongst his disciples. He had often done this before. This time as he did so he said to them:

> 'This is my body, which is given for you. Do this in memory of me.' (Luke 22.19)

Jesus then shared a glass of wine with each of his disciples (picture B). The Passover meal always ended with everyone drinking the 'cup of blessing'. To make

B How does this image remind you of the Church today?

this glass of wine special Jesus said to each of his disciples:

'This is my blood which is poured out for many, my blood which seals God's covenant.' (Mark 14.24)

The bread and the wine

The bread and the wine which Jesus gave to his disciples were symbols:

a The bread symbolised the body of Jesus which was soon to be broken on the cross.

b The wine symbolised the blood of Jesus which was going to be spilt on the cross.

Whenever the followers of Jesus have come together since they have shared bread and wine together in a special service. This service has many names. Roman Catholics call it the Mass; Anglicans call it the Eucharist or Holy Communion; Eastern Orthodox Christians name it the Holy Liturgy whilst in Baptist and Methodist Churches it is called the Lord's Supper or the Breaking of Bread. This service during which Christians remember the death of Jesus is their most important act of worship.

IN THE GLOSSARY

Anglican; Baptist Church; Disciple; Eastern Orthodox Church; Eucharist; Holy Communion; Holy Liturgy; Judas Iscariot; Mass; Passover.

WHAT DO YOU KNOW?

1 a Who betrayed Jesus?

b Who was Jesus betrayed to?

c How does the Passover festival always begin?

d Which Christian service is based on the last meal that Jesus had with his disciples?

2 Imagine that you are a close friend of Judas. Why do you think he decided to betray Jesus?

3 Why do you think that Christians have used bread and wine to keep alive the memory of Jesus for centuries?

3 Death *and* beyond

WASHING FEET

- At the end of his last meal with his disciples Jesus washed their feet.
- Jesus washed their feet to teach them how to be humble.
- Jesus was setting an example for his disciples to follow.

LOOK IN ▶ *John 13.1–17*

Jesus told his disciples at the Last Supper that he was going to be put to death. He gave them the symbols of bread and wine to keep his memory alive after he left earth. One thing remained.

A A woman is anointing the head and body of Jesus. You can read why she is doing this in Matthew 26.6–13.

Jesus, the servant

Travelling in Palestine was a dusty business. Travellers arrived at their destination tired and the lowest servant in the household washed their feet to refresh them. To teach the disciples a lesson Jesus took off his outer cloak and tied a towel around his waist. He poured some water into a basin and began to wash their feet one by one. He dried them with the towel.

The disciples knew that washing feet was the work of servants. Peter, as he often did, gave voice to what the others were thinking. He asked Jesus what he was doing. Jesus told Peter that he could not be a real disciple unless he allowed him to wash his feet. Each disciple, and follower, of Jesus needs to learn to be humble, to give and receive simple acts of kindness. Peter let Jesus continue washing his feet.

The lesson

When Jesus had finished washing their feet he put his cloak back on and returned to his place at the table. He wanted his disciples to know that he had just acted out a parable in front of them. He reminded them that he was their Teacher and Lord – the Son of God. Yet he had been willing to wash their feet. They must now be willing to serve others in the same way:

B Why was the act of Jesus washing the feet of his disciples so surprising?

'I, your Lord and Teacher, have just washed your feet. You, then, should wash one another's feet. I have set an example for you, so that you will do just what I have done for you. I am telling you the truth: slaves are never greater than their master, and messengers are never greater than the one who sent them. Now that you know this truth, how happy you will be if you put it into practice!' (John 13.14–17)

Maundy Thursday

On the Thursday of Holy Week, Maundy Thursday, almost all churches celebrate a special Holy Communion to prepare themselves for the most serious day of the year – Good Friday. During Maundy Thursday this passage about Jesus washing the feet of his disciples is read in church to show how humble Jesus was.

Some churches remember Jesus on this day by copying his actions. Members of the congregation wash each other's feet. This is a reminder to everyone that Christians should serve one another. Sometimes it is only the priest or minister who washes the feet of the congregation. In the Roman Catholic Church it is often the Pope or bishops who wash feet.

IN THE GLOSSARY

Bishop; Disciple; Good Friday; Holy Communion; Holy Week; Maundy Thursday; Minister; Peter; Pope; Priest; Roman Catholic Church.

WHAT DO YOU KNOW?

1 a Which two important things did Jesus do at his last meal with his disciples?
  b Why did Eastern travellers need to have their feet washed? Who usually did it?
  c Who objected to Jesus washing their feet?
  d What did Jesus say to him?
  e On which day do Christians often wash each other's feet today?

2 Imagine that Jesus was on earth today. What do you think he might do to teach his followers humility?

3 Do you think that Christians today might learn a valuable lesson if they had to wash someone else's feet?

BETRAYAL AND ARREST

- Jesus took Peter, James and John with him into the Garden of Gethsemane.
- Jesus prayed three times that he might not have to suffer, but later accepted God's will.
- Judas arrived with a group of soldiers to arrest Jesus.

LOOK IN ▶ *Luke 22.39–53*

After the Last Supper Jesus took three of his disciples (Peter, James and John) with him to a special place – a private garden on the Mount of Olives called Gethsemane. He had probably been there many times before on his own. The mood of Jesus was very sad. He felt that he was fighting all the powers of evil by himself. His friends, though, were not aware of this.

Suffering

To prepare himself for what had to be faced in the next few hours Jesus went on ahead of the disciples. He began to pray to God. He was very frightened by the thought of the future. Although he knew that he could not hope to avoid the suffering he still prayed that some way out might be found by his Father in heaven:

> 'Father, if you will, take this cup of suffering away from me. Not my will, however, but your will be done.' (Luke 22.42)

Three times Jesus returned to his disciples and each time he found them sleeping. By his third visit Jesus knew exactly what God wanted him to do and he was willing to accept it. He woke his disciples up and told them:

> 'Look! The hour has come for the Son of Man [Jesus] to be handed over to the power of sinners.' (Matthew 26.45)

The authorities, led by Judas, had arrived to arrest Jesus. To defend Jesus one of his disciples, Peter, drew a sword and cut off the ear of the High Priest's servant.

A How did the time Jesus spent praying in the Garden strengthen him for the trials ahead?

B Which four events in the life of Jesus are reflected in this banner?

Jesus stopped any further violence and healed the man.

Betrayal

Jesus was arrested by members of the Temple Guard, probably accompanied by one or two Roman soldiers. Judas approached Jesus and kissed him to make sure that the right man was arrested. The kiss was usually a sign of love. Not here though. Sadly Jesus turned to Judas and asked him:

> 'Judas, is it with a kiss that you betray the Son of Man?' (Luke 22.48)

The disciples ran off into the darkness just as Jesus had said they would. The soldiers must have thought about chasing them but they had only been sent to arrest Jesus and they led him away to the house of the High Priest.

Judas soon realised what he had done. He had betrayed the friend with whom he had travelled and talked. They had shared their lives together. Now everything was dark in Judas' life. He went away and hanged himself. His story is one of the saddest in the Bible.

IN THE GLOSSARY
Disciple; High Priest; James; John; Judas; Peter.

WHAT DO YOU KNOW?

1 a Where did Jesus go to pray with his three closest disciples?

b What did Jesus say when Judas arrived?

c How did Judas make sure that the authorities arrested the right man?

d What did the disciples do when Jesus was arrested?

e What happened to Judas?

2 Imagine that you are present in the Garden of Gethsemane when Jesus is arrested. Try to describe the look that you can see on the face of Jesus, and in his eyes, when Judas gives him the kiss of betrayal.

3 Do you think we are being absolutely fair to Judas? Would Jesus have been arrested, tried and executed even if Judas had not betrayed him?

3 Death *and* beyond

ON TRIAL

- The High Priest condemned Jesus to death for blasphemy.
- Pilate, the Roman governor, did not want to condemn Jesus to death.
- The people chose to have Barabbas released and Jesus condemned.

LOOK IN ▶ *Mark 14.53–64*

The Gospels give us slightly different accounts of just what happened on the night before Jesus was put to death. We can, however, put together the sequence of events:

a Jesus stood before Annas, the father-in-law of the High Priest, Caiaphas. Annas had once been High Priest himself. He was curious to find out more about Jesus.

b Jesus before Caiaphas. The Sanhedrin, the Jewish Council, could not meet before dawn. Some members of the Sanhedrin, however, were hurriedly brought together. They asked Jesus several questions. Caiaphas then asked whether he was the Messiah, the Son of God. Jesus replied 'The words are yours'. Caiaphas took this to mean that Jesus was guilty of blasphemy. He tore his clothes, a Jewish sign of great grief.

c Shortly after dawn the full Sanhedrin met. They asked Jesus the same question. Jesus admitted that he was the Messiah. This group, too, found him guilty of blasphemy. It seems, though, that the Sanhedrin could not condemn a person to death. Pontius Pilate, the Roman governor, was the only person who could do that.

d Pilate would not condemn Jesus to death for the 'religious' crime of blasphemy. His opponents, therefore, accused him of other crimes that would interest Pilate:

- misleading the Jewish people
- telling the people not to pay their taxes to Rome
- claiming to be the Jewish leader – the Messiah – who would lead the people against the Romans.

A Who was Pontius Pilate?

B Why was a crown of thorns placed on the head of Jesus after he was condemned by Pilate? You can find the answer by reading Matthew 27.27–29.

Pilate questioned Jesus but could not find any reason to punish him. He wanted to let him go. He tried to solve the problem by falling back on an old Jewish custom. Under this custom the Romans released a prisoner of the people's choice every Passover. Would the people like him to release Jesus? The people demanded that he release Barabbas, a murderer and a thief, who was in prison. This is how Matthew described the choice that the people made:

'The chief priests and the elders persuaded the crowd to ask Pilate to set Barabbas free and have Jesus put to death. But Pilate asked the crowd,

"Which of these two do you want me to set free for you?"
"Barabbas!" they answered.
"What, then, shall I do with Jesus called the Messiah?" Pilate asked them.
"Crucify him!" they all answered.'
(Matthew 27.20–22)

Pilate gave in. He washed his hands in front of the people to show that he did not want to crucify Jesus. He then condemned him to death.

IN THE GLOSSARY
Annas; Blasphemy; Caiaphas; Gospel; High Priest; Matthew; Messiah; Passover; Pontius Pilate; Sanhedrin.

WHAT DO YOU KNOW?

1 a Who was Annas?
  b Who was Caiaphas and why did he condemn Jesus?
  c What opinion did the Sanhedrin have of Jesus?
  d Why was Jesus taken before Pontius Pilate?
  e What did the Jewish leaders accuse Jesus of in front of Pilate?
2 Imagine that you are in the crowd outside Pilate's palace. Do you think you would be amongst those demanding the death of Jesus? Would you keep quiet? Would you have raised your voice against the crowd? Explain your answer.
3 Who do you think was really responsible for the death of Jesus?

3 Death *and* beyond

TO THE CROSS

- Peter denied knowing Jesus three times.
- Jesus was whipped and made to carry his own cross before Simon of Cyrene was brought out of the crowd to help him.
- Today, Christian pilgrims walk up the Via Dolorosa in Jerusalem to remember the death of Jesus.

LOOK IN *Matthew 27.27–31*

Peter denied that he was a disciple of Jesus three times. Twice he was challenged by servant-girls and then by the crowd itself. Each time he denied knowing Jesus. After, remembering the words of Jesus at the Last Supper, he wept bitterly. We know that Jesus later forgave Peter and that he became a leader in the early Church.

Whipping

Pilate condemned Jesus to death, just as the people demanded. The place where criminals were put to death in Jerusalem was a small hill outside the walls of the city called Golgotha. The Romans wanted everyone in the city to be able to see the criminal dying.

As soon as the sentence was passed on Jesus he was whipped. The whip that the Romans used for this had small pieces of bone in the leather straps. Each criminal was lashed 39 times. This was always done to weaken the person as much as possible. Criminals could be on the cross for hours, or even days, before they finally died. Jewish criminals, though, were not allowed to remain on a cross over the Sabbath Day.

To the cross

The cross on which criminals died consisted of two parts:

a The crossbeam was placed across the shoulders of the condemned man and he was made to carry it. This was always very hard as the route to the cross was up-hill all the way. Jesus stumbled several times

A Why were the friends of Jesus only following at a distance at this point?

B Can you think of any other characters, like Simon of Cyrene, who appear very briefly in the story of Jesus?

The Via Dolorosa

The journey that Jesus took to the cross is clearly marked out in Jerusalem today. It is called the Via Dolorosa ('the way of sorrows'). Many pilgrims follow the cobbled road stopping at the places where Jesus stopped, or fell, on his way to the cross. Christians in Jerusalem remember this journey of Jesus each week by taking the same journey following someone carrying a cross. The most popular time for pilgrims to visit the Via Dolorosa is Good Friday. This is the day on which Christians throughout the world remember the death of Jesus. It is the most solemn day of the year for them.

under the weight of the cross. Someone watching, Simon of Cyrene in Africa, was pulled out of the crowd by a soldier and made to carry the cross-beam for Jesus.

b The stem of the cross was taken to the top of the hill by soldiers. The two parts were lashed together by rope.

Crowds lined the road to the cross. Some of them had come to jeer at Jesus and the two other criminals with him. Others were followers of Jesus who could not understand what was happening to him. Amongst those who followed him were his mother, Mary, and another woman also known as Mary.

IN THE GLOSSARY
Disciple; Golgotha; Good Friday; Jerusalem; Mary; Peter; Pontius Pilate; Sabbath Day; Via Dolorosa.

WHAT DO YOU KNOW?

1 a Where were criminals put to death in the city of Jerusalem?

b Why did the Romans try to weaken Jesus as much as possible?

c Who was amongst those who followed Jesus to the cross?

d When do most Christian pilgrims visit Jerusalem to walk up the Via Dolorosa?

e What do Christians throughout the world remember on this day?

2 Imagine you are Peter. How do you think you would have felt after denying Jesus three times? Why did you do it?

3 What might Christians today gain from following in the footsteps of Jesus up the Via Dolorosa?

3 Death *and* beyond

CRUCIFIXION (1)

- **Jesus was crucified between two criminals.**
- **Pilate put a sign above Jesus referring to him as 'the King of the Jews'.**
- **The religious leaders challenged Pilate about the sign but he refused to change it.**

LOOK IN ▶ *John 19.17–24*

Criminals were nailed, or strapped, to a cross and left to die. Their death was very long, extremely painful and full of shame. They were usually stripped naked but Jews, like Jesus, were allowed to wear a loin-cloth on the cross. As Jesus was nailed to his cross so the loss of blood would have made him even weaker. A small wooden ledge underneath his feet

A Read John 19.25–27. John was the 'disciple whom Jesus loved'. How did Jesus tell Mary, his mother, and John to help each other?

allowed him to stand on tip-toe. When he could no longer do this, though, the full weight of his body was taken by his arms and hands. Death, when it came, was by suffocation.

Companions

The Gospels tell us that two other criminals were executed alongside Jesus. We do not know what crimes they committed. They carried their own cross-beams with Jesus up the Via Dolorosa. When Jesus was on the cross some of the crowd mocked and jeered him. The chief priests and other religious leaders pointed out that he had saved others but now seemed unable to save himself. The two criminals also mocked him.

At least, that is what Matthew's Gospel tells us. Luke's Gospel, however, tells a different story. This is how Luke described the scene:

'One of the criminals hanging there hurled insults at him: "Aren't you the Messiah? Save yourself and us."

The other one, however, rebuked him, saying, "Don't you fear God?" You received the same sentence he did … we are getting what we deserve for what we did; but he has done no wrong." And he said to Jesus, "Remember me, Jesus, when you come as King!" ' (Luke 23.39–42)

B Do you think the Gospel writers are trying to say something when they indicate that it was the female followers of Jesus, rather than his disciples, who stayed with him to the end?

Luke also tells how Jesus replied to the repentant criminal:

' "I promise you that today you will be in Paradise with me." ' (Luke 23.43)

The notice

Meanwhile, Pontius Pilate had put a notice above the head of Jesus. This was the thing to do when a criminal was executed. The notice above the head of Jesus simply said:

'This is the King of the Jews.' (Luke 23.38)

Pilate probably did this to annoy the Jewish religious leaders. He knew that they didn't consider Jesus to be their king. The chief priests protested to Pilate and told him he should have written 'This man said, I am the King of the Jews'. Pilate refused to change it. He replied to the religious leaders:

'What I have written, stays written.' (John 19.22)

The soldiers cast lots through dice for the clothes of Jesus at the foot of the cross.

IN THE GLOSSARY
Gospels; Jerusalem; Luke; Matthew; Pontius Pilate.

WHAT DO YOU KNOW?

1 a Who was crucified alongside Jesus?
  b How did the crowd and the chief priests react to Jesus on the cross?
  c How did the two criminals treat Jesus?
  d What did Pilate write on the sign above the head of Jesus?
  e Why did this sign upset the religious leaders so much?
2 Imagine that you are one of the criminals being executed with Jesus. What thoughts are going through your mind as you hang on the cross?
3 How did the repentant thief impress Jesus?

3 Death *and* beyond

CRUCIFIXION (2)

- **Jesus died before the Jewish Sabbath Day began.**
- **The Gospels record seven 'words' that Jesus spoke whilst on the cross.**
- **Christians believe that by celebrating Holy Communion in church they are keeping alive the memory of the death of Jesus.**

LOOK IN ▶ *John 19.28–37*

Certainly Jesus had died, and his body was taken down, before the start of the Sabbath Day. This started at sunset on the Friday evening.

Words from the cross

The Gospels tell us that Jesus spoke seven

A What do Christians believe happened to their sins because of the death of Jesus?

times whilst on the cross and, like the last words of all well-loved people, these words have become very important to Christian believers. They are:

a 'Forgive them Father! They don't know what they are doing.' (Luke 23.34). This was a prayer for the Jewish people and for the Roman soldiers carrying out the execution.

b 'I promise you that today you will be in Paradise with me.' (Luke 23.43). These were the words of Jesus to the repentant thief who was crucified next to him.

c 'He is your son… She is your mother.' (John 19.26–27). These words to his mother, Mary, and to his disciple, John, encouraged them to look after each other in the future.

d 'My God, my God, why did you abandon me?' (Matthew 27.46; Mark 15.34). Jesus was expressing the agony he felt at being separated from God, his Father, and having to carry the burden of the sins of the world.

e 'I am thirsty.' (John 19.28). A jar of white vinegar was beside the cross to dull the pain. A sponge was soaked in it, put on the stem of a hyssop plant and lifted up to Jesus. He drank from it.

f 'It is finished!' (John 19.30). Jesus had completed

B What are Christians doing each time they celebrate Holy Communion together?

the work that he was sent to earth to carry out. He was now ready to die.

g 'Father! In your hands I place my spirit.' (Luke 23.46). Jesus believed, as did all Jews, that God gave new life to a person at birth and took that life away at death.

Bread and wine

Christians believe that the death of Jesus was the climax of his life. He was fulfilling the purpose of God by allowing himself to die on the cross. Through the death of Jesus the sins of all those who believe in him can be forgiven. By his death Jesus paid the price for the sins of the whole world.

It is through the service of Holy Communion that Christians express this belief. The bread on the table reminds them of the body of Jesus which was broken on the cross. The wine is a reminder of the blood of Jesus which was spilt so that sin can be forgiven. As a result a new 'agreement' (covenant) has been made between God and all those who believe. By his death Jesus has given all his followers the gift of eternal life.

IN THE GLOSSARY
Gospels; Holy Communion; John; Mary; Sabbath Day.

WHAT DO YOU KNOW?

1 a Why were the Jews concerned that Jesus should die quickly?

b Who did Jesus ask God to forgive?

c Which two people were told to look after each other after Jesus had died?

d How did Jesus express his agony at feeling separated from God, his Father?

e How was the thirst of Jesus quenched at the very end of his life?

2 Imagine that you had been one of the crowd looking on at the death of Jesus. What do you think might have upset/impressed you most in what you saw?

3 Why do you think the Gospels make it clear that Jesus had to struggle to accept God's will?

3 Death *and* beyond

BURIAL

- Joseph was an important Jew who was probably a secret disciple of Jesus.
- Joseph begged Pilate to let him bury the body of Jesus.
- Joseph laid the body of Jesus in his own unused tomb.

LOOK IN ▶ *Mark 15.42–47*

It seems that Jesus died late in the afternoon on Friday. He was buried in great haste before the Sabbath Day began at sunset.

Joseph of Arithmathea

The story of the burial of Jesus was very important to Mark and his Christian readers. The reason for this is that it emphasised that Jesus had really died.

A What risk was Joseph taking in asking Pilate for the body of Jesus?

This is why Mark tells us that Pilate carefully checked that Jesus had died before releasing the body to Joseph of Arithmathea, a wealthy Jew. Joseph was a member of the Sanhedrin and a loyal Pharisee. Luke's Gospel tells us that Joseph:

> '…was a good and honourable man, who was waiting for the coming of the Kingdom of God. Although he was a member of the Council (Sanhedrin), he had not agreed with their decision and action.' (Luke 23.50–51)

Joseph was a strict Jew. He knew that there were laws to prevent Jews coming into contact with a dead body. The body of a 'criminal' was looked after even more carefully since such people were regarded as 'unclean'. Under Roman law criminals who were executed for treason, as Jesus was, were not even buried. Their bodies were left out in the open to be picked clean by scavenging birds.

Jesus, however, was a Jew. Jewish custom demanded that everyone should be given a proper burial – even criminals. As Jewish custom also determined that no Jewish body should be left on a cross during the Sabbath Day Joseph had to act quickly. We do not know why Joseph became involved in burying the body of Jesus but there are two possible explanations:

a Joseph may have been acting like a good Jew extending the basic kindnesses of life to a fellow Jew.

B What happens on Easter Saturday?

However, Jesus had died just before the start of the Sabbath Day and so there was not time to do this. The women, though, did follow Joseph and so they knew where the body of Jesus had been placed. They then returned home to prepare the oil and spices intending to return as soon as possible after the Sabbath Day had ended.

After Good Friday

Good Friday and Easter Sunday are the two most important days in the Christian calendar. On Good Friday Christians remember the death of Jesus on the cross. On Easter Sunday they celebrate the resurrection of Jesus from the dead.

b Joseph may have been a secret disciple of Jesus who was devastated by the death of Jesus and wanted to give him a decent burial.

Whatever his reason Joseph laid the body of Jesus in his own, unused rock tomb. This may well have been in his own garden since wealthy Jews often built a tomb for themselves and their family there. In the hot climate of Palestine dead bodies were anointed with oil and spices, straight after death, to preserve them as long as possible. This job was carried out by women in the family.

IN THE GLOSSARY
Disciple; Easter Sunday; Good Friday; Mark; Pontius Pilate; Sabbath Day.

WHAT DO YOU KNOW?

1 **a** What do we know about Joseph of Arithmathea?
  b How were the bodies of criminals treated by the Romans?
  c Where did Joseph lay the body of Jesus?
  d Who anointed the bodies of dead people with oils and spices?
  e What do Christians celebrate on Easter Sunday?

2 Imagine that you are one of the early Christians. Why would it be important for you to know that Jesus had been buried in the tomb?

3 What do you think compelled Joseph to bury the body of Jesus at real risk to himself?

3 Death *and* beyond

RESURRECTION

- The women who visited the tomb early on the Sunday morning found that it was empty.
- Angels told the women that Jesus was alive.
- The women returned to tell the news to the disciples but they were not believed.

LOOK IN ▶ *Mark 16.1–8*

All four Gospels have a record of the rising of Jesus from the dead. They do not agree about the details. Remember the first

A Why is the resurrection of Jesus such an important event in the Gospels?

Gospel was not written until at least 35 years after the events it describes. Little wonder that the memories of people had become rather hazy. They all agree, though, that early on the Sunday morning the tomb in which the body of Jesus had been placed was empty.

The angels

Luke's Gospel tells us that two angels, 'two men in bright shining clothes', appeared to the three women who had arrived to anoint the body of Jesus. The angels told the women:

> 'Why are you looking among the dead for one who is alive? He is not here; he has been raised. Remember what he said to you while he was in Galilee: "The Son of Man must be handed over to sinners, be crucified, and three days later rise to life".' (Luke 24.6–7)

The women then remembered the words of Jesus.

Telling the disciples

By this time Judas had hanged himself. The remaining eleven disciples had met together behind locked doors in Jerusalem because they were afraid of being arrested. The women found them and told them what they had seen at the tomb. The women were not

B On which day do Christians today celebrate the resurrection of Jesus?

believed. Peter decided to find out the truth for himself. He ran to the tomb and found the strips of cloth which had been wound around the body of Jesus lying to one side. He did not see any angels and went away wondering what had happened.

In the days following Jesus appeared more than once to his disciples and others. He joined two disciples as they walked along the road to Emmaus. It was only when he split open a loaf in front of them that they realised who their companion was. He appeared to Mary Magdalene who was crying at the tomb because she did not know where the body of Jesus was. He suddenly appeared in a locked room where the disciples were huddled together in fear. He joined his disciples by the Lake of Tiberias where they were unsuccessfully trying to fish. When they did as he told them they caught an immense number of fish. Finally he met with his disciples on a mountainside and told them what he wanted them to do.

Christians today believe that Jesus rose from the dead. They celebrate this in all of their church services. They do so on Easter Sunday in particular.

IN THE GLOSSARY
Angel; Disciple; Gospels; Jerusalem; Mary; Peter.

WHAT DO YOU KNOW?

1 a When was Jesus raised from the dead?

b Who were the first to be told the news about the resurrection of Jesus?

c What did they do next?

d What did Peter do?

e How did Jesus show his disciples that he had risen from the dead?

2 Do you think it is surprising that the four Gospels do not agree in the details of their accounts of the resurrection of Jesus?

3 Imagine that you are one of the disciples. Describe your feelings when you first hear that Jesus has risen from the dead. Do you believe the report or not?

3 Death *and* beyond

ASCENSION

- Jesus appeared to his disciples many times after his resurrection.
- On one occasion he told them what he expected them to do when he had left the earth.
- After blessing his disciples Jesus was taken from them into heaven.

 **LOOK IN** *Matthew 28.16–20*
Luke 24.50–53

The Great Commission

The importance of this appearance of Jesus lay in the words that he had to say to his disciples. He told them that God

A What are we told in Luke's Gospel about Jesus leaving the earth?

had given him all authority (power) in heaven and earth. Because of this he was now telling his disciples to:

> 'Go, then, to all peoples everywhere and make them my disciples: baptize them in the name of the Father, the Son, and the Holy Spirit, and teach them to obey everything I have commanded you. And I will be with you always, to the end of the age.' (Matthew 28.19–20)

The disciples had now been given their work to do. Jesus was shortly going to leave the earth but the disciples would continue his work. They had three tasks:

a To make disciples from all nations of the earth.

b To baptise people in the name of God the Father, the Son and the Holy Spirit.

c To pass on to these new disciples everything that Jesus had taught them.

The Ascension

Luke is the only Gospel writer to tell us how Jesus left the earth. It is a story that he began in his Gospel and completed in the Acts of the Apostles. Jesus took his disciples out of Jerusalem to the outskirts of Bethany, a small village. There he lifted up his hands and blessed

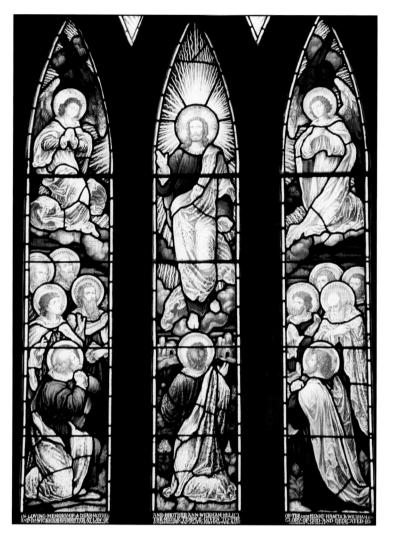

B *Why might some Christians today have a problem with Luke's description of the way Jesus ascended into heaven?*

dressed in white', angels, who told them that the same Jesus who had just left them would return to earth at some future time.

Luke's Gospel tells us that the disciples started worshipping Jesus before returning to Jerusalem with great joy and excitement. When they reached the city they continued to worship God in the Temple.

Ascension Day

Ascension Day is celebrated in some churches. They hold a special Holy Communion service on this day. Those worshipping remember the words of the angels that Jesus will return to the earth.

IN THE GLOSSARY

Acts of the Apostles; Angel; Ascension Day; Baptism; Disciple; Easter Day; Gospels; Holy Communion; Holy Spirit; Jerusalem; Luke.

each of them. It was while he was blessing them that he was taken up into heaven and they could no longer see him. The disciples were joined by 'two men

WHAT DO YOU KNOW?

1 a Where would the new followers of Jesus come from?
  b How must these new followers be encouraged to follow in the footsteps of Jesus?
  c What must the disciples tell the followers of Jesus?
  d Which two books in the New Testament tell the story of the ascension of Jesus?
  e What was Jesus doing when he left his disciples to be taken into heaven?
2 Imagine that you are one of the disciples. Describe your feelings as Jesus is taken away from you.
3 Why were the last words Jesus spoke to his disciples so important? What do they have to do with the Christian Church?

GLOSSARY

A

Abraham — The father of the Jewish nation.

Acts of the Apostles — The book in the New Testament which tells the story of the early Christian Church after Jesus left the earth.

Andrew — One of the disciples, the brother of Peter.

Angel — A being sent from heaven by God to deliver his message.

Anglican — The name of many Churches which are based on the teachings of the Church of England.

Annas — High Priest, the father of Caiaphas who was High Priest at the time of Jesus' arrest.

Apostle — The name given to the disciples after Jesus left the earth.

Aramaic — The language mainly used by Jesus.

Ark — The cupboard in a Jewish synagogue which contains the scrolls on which the Scriptures are written.

Ascension Day — The day on which some Christians celebrate the ascension of Jesus into heaven, 40 days after Easter Day.

B

Baptism — The sprinkling of a person with water to show that their sins have been forgiven.

Baptist Church — A Christian Church that requires all its adult believers to be baptised.

Bar mitzvah — The Jewish ceremony which marks the time when a boy becomes an adult.

Beatitudes — The sayings of Jesus about those people who are truly happy.

Believer's baptism — The practice of the Baptist Church in only baptising adults who believe in Jesus.

Bethlehem — The small village in which Jesus was born.

Bishop — Has authority to conduct confirmations and ordinations. Wears a mitre and carries a crozier.

Blasphemy — Any words spoken against God.

C

Caiaphas — The Jewish High Priest at the time of Jesus' trial.

Circumcision — The Jewish practice of removing the foreskin of a boy's penis when he is eight days old.

D

Devil — The evil power who opposes God, tempted Jesus in the wilderness.

Disciple — A follower of Jesus.

E

Easter Sunday — The day on which Christians celebrate Jesus rising from the dead.

Eastern Orthodox Church — A family of self-governing churches found mainly in eastern Europe. Each church is led by a senior bishop called a Patriarch.

Eucharist — The service at which Christians eat bread and drink wine to remember the death of Jesus.

G

Gentile — A person who is not a Jew.

Golgotha — The place of a skull, the hill on which Jesus was crucified.

Good Friday — The day on which Christians remember the death of Jesus.

Gospels — The four books in the New Testament which tell the story of Jesus.

H

Herod the Great — The ruler of Palestine from 40 to 4 BCE.

High Priest — The leader of the Jews.

Holy Communion — The church service at which Christians remember the death of Jesus.

Holy Liturgy — The name which Orthodox Christians use for Holy Communion.

Holy Spirit — The third member of the Christian Trinity alongside God the Father and God the Son, Jesus Christ.

Holy week — The week in the Christian year that begins with Palm Sunday and ends on Easter Saturday.

I

Infant baptism — The practice of most Christian Churches of baptising babies.

Israel — The country in which Jesus was born.

J

James — Brother of John, one of the disciples.

Jerusalem — The capital of Israel, the place where Jesus died.

John — One of the disciples of Jesus who wrote one of the Gospels.

John the Baptist — Cousin of Jesus, prepared the people for the coming of Jesus.

Joseph — Father of Jesus.

Judas Iscariot — Disciple of Jesus who betrayed him.

L

Lord's Prayer — The prayer that Jesus taught his disciples to use.

Luke — A follower of Jesus who wrote a Gospel and the Acts of the Apostles.

M

Magi — The Eastern astrologers who were guided by a star to the infant Jesus.

Magnificat — The song of Mary after she discovered that she was going to give birth to Jesus.

Mark — A follower of Jesus who wrote one of the Gospels.

Mary — The mother of Jesus.

Mass — The name of the service of Holy Communion in a Roman Catholic Church.

Matthew — A disciple of Jesus who wrote one of the Gospels.

Maundy Thursday — The day before Good Friday.

Messiah — The leader that the Jewish people expected God to send to them.

Minister	A man or a woman who leads the services in a Baptist or Methodist Church.
Miracle	A marvel, an extraordinary event which seems to go against what is known of the laws of nature. To show the love of God, Jesus is said to have performed miracles.
Moses	Great Jewish leader who gave the people the Ten Commandments from God.

N

Nazareth	The area in which Jesus grew up.
New Testament	The part of the Bible which contains the four Gospels.

P

Palestine	The country in which the events in the Gospels took place, also known as Israel.
Palm Sunday	The day on which Christians remember the entry of Jesus into Jerusalem.
Parable	A story told by Jesus to teach an important spiritual lesson.
Passover	The Jewish festival which looks back to the time when God released the slaves from Egypt.
Peter	The leading disciple of Jesus, brother of Andrew.
Pharisee	A member of a strict Jewish religious group.
Pontius Pilate	The Roman governor of Judea between 26 and 36 CE who sentenced Jesus to death.
Pope	The leader of the world's Roman Catholics.
Priest	A person who leads the worship in Roman Catholic, Anglican and Orthodox Churches.
Prophet	A person who speaks God's message.
Protestant	A Christian who does not belong to either the Orthodox or Roman Catholic Churches.

R

Rabbi	A Jewish teacher.
Roman Catholic Church	The community of Christians throughout the world which follows the leadership of the Pope, as the successor of St Peter on earth.

S

Sabbath Day	The Jewish holy day when no work can be done.
Sadducee	A member of an important religious group at the time of Jesus.
Samaritan	Descendants of people who lived in Samaria.
Sanhedrin	The Jewish Council which played a part in the death of Jesus.
Satan	Another name for the Devil.
Scribe	A Jewish scholar.
Sermon on the Mount	Most important collection of the teachings of Jesus.
Shema	The Jewish name for the words recorded in Deuteronomy 6.4. This statement of belief stands at the very heart of the Jewish faith and is still recited in Jewish homes and in the synagogue.
Synagogue	A Jewish meeting place, place for education and worship.

T

Temple	The centre of Jewish worship in Jerusalem.
Ten Commandments	Laws which were given by God to Moses on Mount Sinai (Exodus 20.1–17).
Torah	The Jewish law, the first five books of the Old Testament.

V

Via Dolorosa	The way of sorrows, the road that Jesus took to the cross.

Z

Zealots	A small Jewish group dedicated to forcing the Romans out of Palestine.